Discover Your Windows

Lining Up with God's Vision

Kent R. Hunter

Abingdon Press
Nashville

DISCOVER YOUR WINDOWS: LINING UP WITH GOD'S VISION
Copyright © 2002 By Abingdon Press
All rights reserved.

This book is printed on acid-free paper.

ISBN 0-687-02154-5
ISBN-13: 978-0-687-02154-3

Scripture quotations, unless otherwise indicated, are from the New Revised Standard Version of the Bible, copyright © 1989, by the Division of Christian Education of the National Council of the Churches of Christ in the United States of America. Used by permission. All rights reserved.

08 09 10 11—10 9 8 7 6

MANUFACTURED IN THE UNITED STATES OF AMERICA

Dedicated to

Robert Shaw
Bob Grimm
Kari Grimm
Barbara Grimm
Mike Friend
Nancy Friend

Big picture thinkers
with a heart for God

Acknowledgments

Every book has an army of people standing behind the author. Books are major projects that include many people way beyond the person whose name is on the book.

For this project, at the front of this army stands Kelly Hahn, my writing assistant and staff writer for Church Doctor Ministries. This book has been a journey for Kelly, and he has traveled it very well.

I am also thankful for our team at Church Doctor Ministries: Neil Bachman, Michael Brown, Elaine Cobbs, Tom Hamel, Olive   Hinkley, Shelly Hinkley, Heather Jones, Michelle Jones, Adam Kroemer, Kenton Morton, Everaldo Rego, Carissa Ross, Roberta Stroh, Barry Kolb and Neil Kanning.

I would also like to thank Rebecca Blevins, Lisa Ellis, Evelyn Gibson, John Hinkley, Janet Hunter, Melissa Montana, Al Pownell, Bob Whitesel, John Williamson, Sid Pepe, and Don Wunrow—just a few of the many incredible people who have assisted Church Doctor Ministries in various creative capacities.

I am also grateful for our Board of Directors—a group of extraordinary Christians who see through windows that stretch the horizons of what God has in mind for Christians today: Brad Benbow, Jerry Boyers, Paul Griebel, Jim Manthei, Roger Miller, Rob Olson, Greg Ulmer, Wayne Register, and Nels Umble.

I am particularly grateful for the special encouragement I have received about the value of worldviews in the Christian's life from Chuck Colson, Darrow Miller, and Jim Manthei.

As I have mentioned with every book project, my family continues to stand by me and support a husband and dad who travels frequently and has more book projects than a person could accomplish in three lifetimes. My gratitude to my great partner in life, Janet, our daughter Laura, and son Jon.

Finally, I want to express my deep appreciation to the hundreds of churches that have given us the privilege of serving them through the consultation efforts of Church Doctor Ministries. We have become partners and friends with those we have served, and it is great to see the incredible changes that have taken place as the Lord's work reaches new levels in these congregations. There is no question that the reason I have been born, the reason I am on this earth, is to help churches, one Christian at a time. Our deep thanks to the 15,000 people who sat in one-half-hour to one-hour interviews and to the 18,000 people who completed questionnaires that provide the basis for the amazing insights we have gained and shared in this book. Those discoveries will reshape the thinking and behavior of thousands of readers who will never look through old windows again.

Contents

Preface

I visited a church the week before the grand opening of its new worship center. Many aspects of the building were considerably upgraded for the contemporary worship service. The architect and building committee had made a valiant attempt to provide a welcome center. As I looked at this new building, the evangelism director asked what I thought about the welcome center. My heart ached as I had to tell the truth. It was at the wrong end of the lobby!

The architect had positioned the building between a street and the parking lot. Unfortunately, he had a worldview from the 1950s, when most people walked to churches designed to serve neighborhoods. In the twenty-first century, people drive to church and parking lots determine people flow. In the drawing stage, the welcome center could have easily been positioned so guests would encounter the welcome center. Now that the building was built, it would be almost impossible to change. What happened? The architect was working with a worldview that no longer made sense. It was no longer relevant to the world in which we now live.

There is no question about it: Your worldview drives your behavior. Many in churches are asked to make decisions or provide opinions. The topic doesn't matter; there are always others who disagree. Why? Because they operate out of a different worldview, look out different windows. Churches are often divided because people see things differently.

The church is God's creation. He has put people like you and me in it to do the work he has a passion to complete. My assumption is that if you see the world the way God sees it, you will be more united and productive for what God wants to accomplish. Collectively, Christians will be part of a church that powerfully impacts the lives of people in their community.

This book is not about theory. It is based on significant research. We have discovered ten windows that can help you become more productive for God. It's our assumption that you want to be all God intended you to be. As you review these ten windows, they will affect the way you see your world. That, in turn, will direct the way you form your opinions, make your decisions, and the way you conduct yourself.

The research is based on large numbers of people who are active in their churches—but who demonstrate unbiblical worldviews. Most of them don't even know it.

This book is your personal compass. It will help you discover the way you see the world and how you understand the way the world works. Your mirror will be how God sees the world according to the Bible. Look through these windows, and you will see your behavior change. As you direct others to these windows, you will also see your church undergo a transformation. Worldview issues are behind all the other issues. You will move from symptom solving to the causative issues you wrestle with every day. Share these windows with your Sunday school class, small group, ministry team, committee or board. It will help you get on the same page and become a powerful church for God in this world.

Biblical windows will change your church from the inside out—because the way you look through your window drives your behavior. Your worldview, once changed, will change your life from the inside out.

At the end of each window-chapter, there is a section called "Getting a Better View". This is for discussion and processing. That's how people change. It's how you will change. Share it with others and it's how your church will change. And you will never be the same!

KENT R. HUNTER
The Church Doctor
Corunna, Indiana

Worldview: Not Another Program!

"Sometimes you have to see things differently in order to do things differently."
General Electric advertisement

A number of years ago, my wife and I lived for fourteen months in Australia. Prior to our arrival, a few friends told us that in Australia, the water goes down the drain in a different direction. I thought they were pulling my leg! So when we arrived in Sydney, I went straight to the first restroom I could find and flushed the toilet. Sure enough—the water went down the other way! I learned later that this is due to the Coriolis Effect—the spin of the earth. Living in another country forced me to see that the world really doesn't revolve around me, my country, my little town, or my assumptions about the way the world works. My *worldview* was beginning to change. As the day was ending, I scanned the night sky for the Big Dipper. I couldn't find it anywhere. It was then that I realized that people in the southern hemisphere don't see the same sky I had seen my whole life. Now I found myself looking at the Southern Cross for the first time. My *worldview* was changing again.

Among the many wall decorations in my office is a map of the world. It's like most world maps, except Australia is at the top of the map and the United States and Canada are at the bottom. The tips of Africa and South America appear at the top, but Russia, China, Iceland, and Greenland all appear at the bottom. I love that map, because it symbolizes what our ministry does best—helping people see the world in ways they've never seen it before.

Sometimes when visitors are in my office, they'll raise their eyebrows in the direction of the map and say something like, "Why is your map upside down?" I usually respond by saying, "It all depends on your perspective. It may look wrong to you because you live in the northern hemisphere, but what if you were from the southern hemisphere? Wouldn't you be inclined to look at the world *this* way?" Already, my visitors are beginning to see the world differently. They have been introduced to what Church Doctor Ministries is all about.

Your worldview is the window through which you see the world and understand the way the world works. *More than anything else, your worldview impacts your behavior toward this world.* Worldviews are shaped by countless immeasurable factors in your life, and are generally sub-conscious. As Darrow Miller puts it, "All of us wear a set of lenses in our minds, but few of us are aware of their presence."[1]

Today, the Internet is changing our worldview daily. Up-to-date information about other cultures is only a few clicks away. Years ago, people waited for the nightly news to update events that had transpired during the day. Now, it's posted on the Internet within a matter of minutes. Stock traders can scrutinize quotes and then buy or sell—all from their computer.

I remember a General Electric ad that appeared in *Time* magazine years ago. It simply, but profoundly, said, "Sometimes you have to see things differently in order to do things differently." It's undeniably true, and more than anything else, it's exactly what needs to happen to today's Christians.

If your church is plateaued or declining . . . if your church has tensions and difficulties . . . if you think worship is boring . . . if unchurched people think your church is irrelevant . . . if your church is not helping you to grow spiritually . . . chances are you and your church need to do some things differently. However, in order to do things differently, you need to see things differently. Seeing things differently means processing everything through a biblical window. How you see your church makes all the difference.

For the past almost thirty years, those of us at Church Doctor Ministries have been helping churches. We use the "Church Doctor" concept intentionally. It's based on our understanding of the Scripture that the church is not just a building or an institution. It is a living organism that, when healthy, breathes, moves, and grows. When sick, it stagnates, erodes, and dies. Throughout the New Testament, the Scripture uses many metaphors to describe what we call the church. Whether it's the vine and the branches, the royal priesthood, the fellowship of believers, the family of God, the kingdom of God, the sheep and the shepherd—they all express a dynamic, fluid, living organism. One of the most poignant descriptions is that of the church as the body of Christ. When I first discovered that the Bible calls the church something other than a building, a place, or an organization, it gave me a new window of understanding through which to see the church.

As Church Doctors, our team evaluates the health and vitality of churches. Using an agenda much like medical doctors, we follow a similar approach of diagnosis, prognosis, and prescription. The first step, *diagnosis*, analyzes the symptoms and determines the real challenge. We do this by engaging a process of elimination to discover the causative issues of ill health and lack of productivity. Once the diagnosis is made, we employ the discipline of *prognosis*—predicting the probable direction and life of the church given the present set of circumstances, or a change of circumstances. The diagnosis and prognosis bring to light issues that are hindering growth and effectiveness in the church. From there, we practice the art of *prescription*—providing recommendations and suggestions that lead to recovery and vitality. Most physicians recognize that they don't cure the human body. They provide favorable circumstances through treatments and recommendations so that God's great creation, the human body, can cure itself. They remove roadblocks that allow the sicknesses to take over the body. Sometimes it can be done by medical manipulation, but other times it requires surgery.

Likewise, when it comes to the body of Christ, we recognize that God is the one who brings health and vitality to the church. Our mission involves removing roadblocks in the church so that God can be God, and move churches to health and productivity.

In the diagnostic process, we've identified numerous symptoms that indicate the presence of a larger issue. Dwindling attendance in Bible classes; high levels of gossip in a congregation; widespread apathy; weak financial support; all these are symptoms.

Most church leaders are eager to find a program that will help their church. Unfortunately, most programs target symptoms. Effective programs treat conditions by trying to incorporate fellowship, get people into the Bible, and enhance worship. But real productivity with the potential to affect lives and make a difference in communities, requires getting beyond the symptoms to the causative issue(s). The real issue(s) can always be traced back to people like you and me. That's why, at Church Doctor Ministries, we say, "we help churches one Christian at a time."

During a recent research project, we gathered information from written questionaires that were part of a targeted study sent to over 18,000 people who were actively involved in their churches. Then, to discover the causative issues at a deeper level, we interviewed over 15,000 of these church members. With the data from these interviews, we have identified symptoms that manifest themselves within the body and thwart potential. More important, we have also identified the causative issues behind the symptoms. *From this we have identified and isolated ten basic worldviews that are in conflict with the biblical worldviews of how the church should function.*[2] They are held by large numbers of influencers and decision-makers in churches. While some members of the church process issues through a biblical window, many do not. Therein lies the real tension behind the struggles church leaders, pastors, staff, and members are challenged with every day.

What about you? What are your worldviews in your approach to church? By the time you finish this book, you will self-diagnose ten core values that make or break a healthy church life. Some may surprise you. Some may challenge you to change. If you do, you'll be a different person. If you help others through the process, you'll have a different church. You'll discover that the "problems" you have identified in the past and worked so hard to correct are not the problems at all! They are merely the symptoms.

The issues behind the issues are manifested in the way you see the church, and how you understand the way it works. Improving the church is an inside job. Chuck Colson said, "Our choices are shaped by what we believe is real and true, right and wrong, good and beautiful. Our choices are shaped by our worldview."[3] Your worldview is the window through which you see your world. Affecting the world begins with you—and your windows—because your worldview drives your behavior.

> The "problems" you have identified in the past and worked so hard to correct are not the problems at all! They are merely the symptoms.

When Jesus taught about the kingdom, he shaped and fashioned a worldview about what it meant to be a Christian. Because of this, much of his teaching directly contrasted the worldview of the religious leaders of his day. He warned people to look out for the "yeast of the Pharisees" (Matthew 16:6)—which was the way the Pharisees looked at the world and how it worked. This was usually in conflict when it pertained to their spiritual lives.

Worldview issues are at the heart of meaningful reform and renewal of the local church. Too often, churches resemble the man who was rapidly killing flies with a flyswatter—all the while neglecting to shut the kitchen door. Pastors and church leaders become fatigued putting out fires, but fail to take the matches away from those who are starting them. In your church life, ever feel like you're hitting your head against a brick wall? Many Christians spend their lives battling symptoms, and wonder why they have not effected real change.

The ten biblical windows we have isolated are worldviews that drive behavior. They help or hinder what God intends to accomplish through you. Here are the ten windows, and their opposites. As a Christian, how do you see your world?

WINDOW	BIBLICAL WORLDVIEW	OPPOSING WORLDVIEW
The Window of Purpose	The main purpose of Christians in the church is to make disciples	The main purpose of Christians in the church is to provide a place of fellowship and share God's love with each other
The Window of Comfort	God is more interested in your character than in your comfort	You want comfort at all costs
The Window of Image	You are to go to the world	You expect the world to come to you
The Window of Priorities	You want God's will to be done above everything else	Your own priorities are more important than God's
The Window of Stewardship	You give back from God's blessings	You give to the church budget

The Window of Financing	You believe God pays for what he orders	You ask, "How much does it cost?"
The Window of Change	You're encouraged by tradition: the living faith of the dead	You're caught in traditionalism: the dead faith of the living
The Window of Leadership	You expect your pastor to train you for ministry	You believe your pastor is hired to do ministry for you
The Window of Teamwork	Your spiritual gifts empower you for God's work	You serve because you've been drafted or elected
The Window of Attitude	You know God can	You believe God can't

Identifying the vitality and effectiveness of the church, Tommy Tenney writes, "True church growth . . . wherever it may be springs forth from an intimate knowledge of the living God."[4] This book will help you see a different sky—a biblical perspective of what it means for you to be the church. It will empower you to cure symptoms, solve problems, and more effectively work toward the fulfillment of the Great Commission. My goal? That you will never be the same!

Your Purpose Determines Your Mission

"I think the main purpose of the church is to have fellowship with my friends."

In the Huddle

"Have you heard what our pastor has gone and done now? He's just decided to preach without wearing his robe. I don't remember having a vote on that. Besides that, have you heard that noise the choir is singing these days? I don't know what's gotten into them. What happened to all those songs that we're used to—the ones *we* like? You know, I had to attend that trustees meeting the other night. It went on forever. I bet we argued for three hours. Jim is trying to get speed bumps put in the drive around the parking lot. Whoever heard of such a silly notion? Do you know what that'll cost?"

Ever say anything like that at your church? Do petty squabbles receive too much attention? Do you have a tendency to major in the minors? Why is there so much turmoil in the church today? How can you concentrate on the crucial issues and avoid being plagued by peripherals?

When I was in high school, I played football. If you've never played football, imagine for a moment what it might be like in the huddle—late in the fourth quarter. Think about how the players might smell. As they gather in that closeness of the huddle, consider what their breath might be like. How do you think their uniforms look? Nothing but dirt, sweat, and unpleasant smells everywhere, yet in all the huddles I was ever in, I never heard anybody say, "Hey Joe, tuck in your shirt, you look sloppy! Or what about you, Fred . . . you've got all those grass stains on the front of your pants! Man,

Jerry, your breath is terrible. Adam, did you put on *any* deodorant?"

Why are these comments never heard in the middle of a huddle late in the fourth quarter? Because they're irrelevant and insignificant! Football teams are driven by their goal—to win the game. They're riveted in their attention and united in their action. They understand why they're on the field, and what they want to accomplish. They're focused on their purpose.

How does this relate to your church life? Well, churches aren't much different than the football team I described. Your church also has a purpose. That purpose is the reason it exists. The Bible says your church exists to reach people with the life-saving message of the gospel. Everyday people die without a relationship with Jesus Christ, who paid for their sins with his death and resurrection. Ever since the church began, it's been late in the fourth quarter, because Jesus never said when the end will come! "But about that day and hour no one knows, neither the angels of heaven, nor the Son, but only the Father" (Matthew 24:36). Years later, when he was writing to the church in Thessalonica, the Apostle Paul would echo Jesus' words. "Now concerning the times and the seasons, brothers and sisters, you do not need to have anything written to you. For you yourselves know very well that the day of the Lord will come like a thief in the night" (1 Thessalonians 5:1-2). There's a profound sense of urgency to spread the gospel message. For people worldwide, eternity hangs in the balance. Like Carl F. H. Henry said, "The gospel is good news only if it arrives in time." Today is the last day for someone!

> *Ever since the church began,*
> *it's been late in the fourth quarter.*

But when you aren't focused on the primary purpose, you have a tendency to become focused on everything else.

That's missing the point! It reminds me of the story of three monks who were only allowed to speak once a year. On the appointed day, one monk said, "I wish we could have seeds in our rye bread." A year went by, and the day came around again. A different monk said, "I prefer rye bread without seeds." The following year, the third monk remarked, "I can't stand this constant bickering!"[1]

What would happen if everything you complained about was viewed according to how much difference it would ultimately make in God's kingdom? Would it still seem worth creating turmoil? Would it still seem important enough to argue about instead of reaching the lost?

The Restroom Debate

At St. Matthew Community Church, an ugly debate broke out concerning the only restrooms in the building. They were located in the basement, and many older members had difficulty navigating the stairs. Built twenty years earlier, they had been repaired and repainted several times. Now they were in such a state of deterioration that it was nearly impossible to keep them clean. Nothing about them looked sanitary or inviting.

Several members began a campaign to renovate. Their belief was that visitors who saw the church's restrooms would be unlikely to return. They were *that* embarrassing. The members proposed a plan to build new restrooms, accessible from the sanctuary. To convenience everyone, the new restrooms would be equipped with baby changing tables, as well as facilities for children and the disabled. They felt it was a solid plan with a purpose to communicate sensitivity to worshippers.

Much to their surprise, some of their good friends at St. Matthew balked at the idea. A few contradicted the belief that restrooms should look modern. They seemed to be acceptable to most of the members. Honestly, if visitors didn't return based on the appearance of the restrooms, did they really *want* them to come back? Others who opposed the proposal held differing views on where and how the church's money should be spent. They argued that the expense to renovate the restrooms was unfeasible. Other programs in the church were higher priorities.

But the restrooms were never the real issue. The real issue behind the argument was the perspective and understanding of the primary purpose of the church. Those who opposed the idea on the grounds of personal opinion viewed the purpose of the church as maintaining a nice, comfortable atmosphere for those who already belonged to the church. The window through which they saw the main purpose of the church faced inwardly. Those who felt the need to renovate for visitors believed the church exists to reach those *outside* the church. The window through which they saw the main purpose of the church faced outwardly. The argument occurred because two different belief systems were clashing. The real problem was that one group held a biblical worldview of the main purpose of the church, and the other group held a different worldview. The visible symptom of the deeper problem was an eruption over restroom renovation.

FIGURE 1A

SYMPTOM

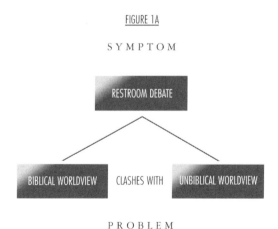

PROBLEM

When the church is united in its purpose, it's less likely to focus on trivial issues. You don't get hung up on the speed bumps of church life. You don't sweat the small stuff when you "huddle" for meetings or activities. There's no need to major in minors because the purpose is top priority! When time, energy, and focus are dedicated to the primary purpose, the church is healthy and productive. So are you!

So Who Was Right?

What is the primary purpose of the church? Were those campaigning for new restrooms wrong in wanting to spend money to impress outsiders instead of spending it on programs for those already in the church? Were those who opposed the proposal wrong for having a differing belief on the importance of modern restrooms? I've alluded to the answer, but let's hear it from the mouth of the church's CEO: Jesus Christ.

Jesus gave important instructions to his disciples after his resurrection. Those twelve were the foundation of the first-century church. Throughout his three-year ministry, he had groomed them to take the gospel message to the world. Now, that time had come. At the end of Matthew's gospel, Jesus says to his disciples, "All authority in heaven and on earth has been given to me. Go therefore and make disciples of all nations, baptizing them in the name of the Father and of the Son and of the Holy Spirit, and teaching them to obey everything I have commanded you. And remember, I am with you always, to the end of the age" (Matthew 28:18-20).

The key objective in Jesus' charge is "make disciples." He never intended for it to become an option. He didn't say, "If you have time," or, "It'd be great if you . . ." He said, "make disciples of all nations." That commission also never implied a timeframe. There was no statute of limitations given for how long the church needs to make disciples. His command begins with the participle, "go," and only the faintest hint of closure surrounds the words, "to the end of the age," which has yet to occur. Jesus commissioned his followers to go and make disciples, and has never told us to stop. When you look through the biblical window, the view is clear: the main purpose of the church is to make disciples. Visitors count . . . and so do clean restrooms that encourage them to come back.

But over centuries, this biblical worldview for the primary purpose of the church has been altered—although never by Jesus. It's been altered by human opinion.

If seeing things differently helps you to do things differently, then viewing the main purpose of the church through a biblical window is the first step toward becoming an effective Christian. If you don't have Christ's perspective on the purpose of his church, the less important issues will be equally, or more drastically, skewed. The reason? How you see your purpose determines your mission.

By the Numbers

Most Christians are familiar with Christ's Great Commission, so why do so many churches still wind up putting out fires instead of being "on fire?" Are the squabbles a result of a few select members with unbiblical worldviews stirring up dissent? The responses to our Mission Awareness Survey[2] give insight to how Christians see the window of purpose. It says, "Pick from the following statements the one that best describes the main purpose of the church." The survey shows the following options:

A. Teach the golden rule
B. Be the moral backbone of society
C. Make disciples
D. To provide a place of fellowship and share God's love with one another

Which one would you choose?

The research data reveals that only 3.4% of those surveyed believe the main purpose of the church is to act as the moral backbone of society, and 4.1% advocated that the church's main priority should be to teach the Golden Rule.

That leaves a majority of those surveyed with one of two answers. Of the remaining 92% of church members surveyed, 57% of individuals believe the main purpose of the church is to provide a place of fellowship and share God's love *with one another*. This is where many of those at St. Matthew who opposed the restroom renovations would fall. Their perception was that since the restrooms seemed fine to the members, why renovate?

But this answer doesn't line up with Jesus Christ's Great Commission. If the church's main responsibility and purpose on earth is to provide a designated place for people to fellow-

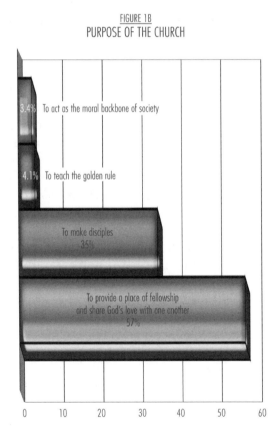

FIGURE 1B
PURPOSE OF THE CHURCH

ship together, where is the outreach? How are unbelievers added to God's family? How can they hear the gospel message and then consider the claims of Christ? How do people go from darkness to light? How do people avoid hell if they were not born into a Christian family and brought up in a Christian home?

The Country Club Church

Fellowship is essential to the body of Christ. Growing spiritually with other Christians fosters a healthy community. Perhaps you've heard someone say, "A Christian without a church is an orphan." It's true! A strong sense of fellowship creates unity and a healthy base for the church to accomplish its mission of reaching others. As important as it is, fellowship is not the main purpose of the church.

In the Holy Land, the Sea of Galilee receives water from the Jordan River. The sea is healthy and vibrant and supports farming in villages all around it. From there, the water flows into the Dead Sea, where it just stops. There's no outlet. And it *is* dead. Healthy churches are balanced churches. The biblical window of making disciples includes a balance between fellowship and outreach. Both are essential for the health and vitality of a church. A church that operates under the assumption that the purpose of the church is to share God's love with those already in the church resembles the Dead Sea. It's self-contained. It doesn't go anywhere. It's stagnant. As the old saying goes, "Impression without expression leads to repression." How you see your purpose determines your mission. If a church's purpose is to create a fellowship atmosphere among members, the mission will revolve around a maintenance mentality. But if a church's purpose is to make disciples, the mission will revolve around others. Upgraded restrooms matter to new people . . . who matter to God.

Think about country clubs. Members pay dues to receive numerous amenities. Different kinds of people belong to country clubs. Some wholly expect to be served, and others help with various club functions. The purpose of the country club is to make the members happy and comfortable with the reciprocated expectation that they will continue to be members and pay dues to cover the bills. That's the design of a country club, and there really isn't anything wrong with that in itself. But it's not the intended design for the church. The purpose of a country club church is to keep those *already* in the church content and satisfied. When that happens, outreach is almost always put on the back burner because the programs, expenditures, and functions are usually aimed at meeting the members' needs.

The argument over restrooms at St. Matthew Community Church is a symptom of people who lack a biblical perspective. Whether the issues involve restrooms, carpet colors, building additions, or worship services, the underlying problem is the result of seeing the purpose of the church through the wrong window. Someone once said, "The world at its worst needs the church at its best." The church has plenty to offer a world sliding farther from God. Jesus never asked anyone to come up with a different or better plan. He commissioned us to carry out the main purpose of the church. Through a biblical window, that means making disciples. Through another window, it could mean anything, because one thing's for sure: how you see your purpose really does determine your mission.

Lining up the Windows

Window 1:   Your Purpose Determines Your Mission

Getting a Better View

1. You can't have a biblical worldview without being in the Bible! The best way for you to get reacquainted with the purpose of the church is to join a small group and study the images describing the church in the New Testament. Use the small group study *Six Faces of the Christian Church*[3] to start thinking and talking about God's main purpose for the church.

2. A way to promote the clarity of purpose at your church is to encourage your pastor to preach and teach on the Great Commission goal. Study the priorities reflected by Jesus during His time on earth. Why did He die on the cross? What did He mean when he said to His followers, "As the Father has sent me, so I send you?" Why is it that Jesus reserved His last words on earth to focus on witnessing (Acts 1:8)? What is your church's *mission*?

3. Take a field trip to a healthy, growing church in your area. Visit with the staff and key leaders. Ask them what they perceive to be the primary purpose of their church. Do a simple research study in your own congregation, asking people what they perceive to be the primary purpose of the church.

4. Review the purpose statement of your constitution. What does it say about the primary purpose of your church? How is that reflected in the budget, or how the leaders and members spend their time? Filter every discussion, every agenda, and every meeting through the purpose of your church. Review your church's mission statement. How does it match up with the biblical purpose of the church? If your church doesn't have one, make it a high priority to draft one. I've written a book on how to create a biblical mission statement for your church,[4] or hire an outside consultant to help your church revise it's mission statement or constitution.

5. What does your church life reflect as your window of purpose? Get together with others and look at the windows in this book. Ask your leaders to study this book together as well as the book of Acts. Based on the actions displayed by the apostles and others, through which window were they looking at the world? What did they see as their main purpose as the people of God?

The Last Word

"Jesus founded the church, died for the church, sent his Spirit to the church, and will someday return for his church. As the owner of the church, he has already established the purposes, and they're not negotiable."[5]

Rick Warren

Your Comfort Determines Your Sacrifice

"I visited this church and joined because I found it to be comfortable."

A Bad Day for Art

Put yourself in my shoes: You've worked hours to craft and perfect a sermon message. You've really done your homework. You've spent hours praying about it. Now, just minutes before worship, you're mentally, spiritually, and emotionally prepared to preach a life-changing message.

Art approached me just as I was about to enter the sanctuary . . . and he was clearly not happy. His face was a suffused red, and his hands were clenching and unclenching.

"Pastor, *you're* responsible for bringing all these new people into this church! You seem to think all this growth is a good thing. Now there's somebody parked in my parking spot!" I thought for a moment—that's right—Art's the one who parks under the only shade tree in the entire parking lot. Everybody who's been a member knows that. And rather than deal with Art, they just let him park there. But some unknowing, ignorant newcomer, accidentally parked in his spot.

I looked at Art, glanced out at the sanctuary, and then looked at Art again. I sighed and said, "Art, I think you're going to have a really bad day." Art looked confused.

"Why is that, pastor?" he responded.

"Because," I said, "I think they're also sitting in your pew!"

I probably enjoyed that a bit more than I should have as a pastor. But Art was one of those people who consistently put *comfort* above *cross*. He was unwilling to make sacrifices for the good of others. But Art isn't alone in that category. It's a root problem in the church that manifests itself in symptoms of selfishness. Few people recognize it because it's subtly embedded—it doesn't stand out where it can be noticed. No one would ever stand up at a meeting and say, "Whatever we decide, it should speak to the issue of my comfort more than anything else." You'd be crazy to say that! Instead, the problem is hidden behind a smokescreen of pious platitudes and good intentions. The truth is, many Christians have a consumer approach to the church—one that allows them to avoid stretching—one that ignores the roughness of the cross—one that preserves comfort at all costs.

Consumerism in the Church

Ever hear anything like this in your church?

"I don't know about you, but I'm not happy with that new music they're playing in church. I think they're just trying to entertain some of those young outsiders. Why, those people don't even know how to act in church. *I* feel like an outsider in church these days. I'm not comfortable with that new music. In my opinion it's disrespectful to God—with all that noise, it has to be. I don't see why we have to do things for *them*. It's our church! When I come to church, I want peace and tranquility. Those people who've turned our worship of God into a rock and roll concert just upset me. It's not peaceful at all!"

That's the perspective of an ecclesiastical consumer. The complaint sounded like an objection to different music, but it was presented with the words, "It's disrespectful to God." That opposition, especially couched within such a pious-sounding objection is a symptom of the larger problem—the obsession with comfort.

Just recently I saw an advertisement for a credit card with a $50,000 credit line. The picture next to the ad showed a man sprawled on a hammock near the shore of a tropical island. That picture of comfort is an effective pull that encourages consumers to buy into such a fantasy. We live in a consumer driven society. Businesses offer several options and varieties of the same product. We've come to expect it, and it's a great way to run an economy! It's a lousy way to run a church. Talking to one of the churches he oversaw, Paul said, "Do nothing from selfish ambition or conceit, but in humility regard others as better than yourselves. Let each of you look not to your own interests, but to the interests of others" (Philippians 2:3-4). Paul then points to Christ as the model of someone whose comfort was not a priority. Although Christ was God in the flesh, he never demanded his rights as God. Instead, he served the world in complete humility and submitted himself to a brutal death by crucifixion. He spent his whole life considering the needs of others more than his own. Not just the people who shared the planet with him at the time—but people he'd never met. He regarded everyone to be better than himself: from the grocer on the corner to the CEO of the world's largest business to the homeless man on the street. That perfect humility led Jesus to a cross.

Jesus didn't wait until Calvary to put cross above comfort. His teachings, backed up by his life, demonstrated He was always willing to sacrifice for others. Once, Jesus had a man approach him and ask if he could be his follower. Jesus gave a strange response. He said, "Foxes have holes, and the birds of the air have nests; but the Son of Man has nowhere to lay his head" (Matthew 8:20). What he was saying was that while the rest of the world was comfortable in bed, the Son of Man was on a journey that often put him among the homeless. Jesus also said "Those who find their life will lose it, and those who lose their life for my sake will find it" (Matthew 10:39) and, "whoever does not take up the cross and follow me is not worthy of me" (Matthew 10:38). Jesus makes it clear that sacrifice is essential to being his follower. It's even more essential to being a Christian leader. Gail Sheehy said,

"Growth demands a temporary surrender of security." Sacrificing comfort indicates a dedication to growth.

Through Which Window Are You Looking?

The window through which you see your comfort determines how much you will sacrifice. It's a window with eternal implications. If Christians value comfort above sacrifice, their church's "needs" will show it. The needs will benefit those already in the church, but will give little regard to those on the outside. You won't find it on any documents or mission statements, but it will be evident in your church's budget, mission awareness, outreach efforts, ministry training, tolerance for varieties of worship, and financial vitality. Some members say they aren't comfortable with witnessing to others because the fear of rejection makes them uncomfortable. Some are against contemporary worship because they're more comfortable with a traditional style. Some Christians wince when they're challenged to stretch financially for God's work. They're used to giving what makes the checkbook comfortable.

Comfort-first is short-sighted and uninvolved in reaching the lost or maturing the Christian in discipleship. How high of a priority is your comfort? Do you subordinate your comfort to the cause of Christ? Is your pastor more concerned with keeping members content than rocking the boat and getting kingdom work done? If so, you're heading toward an avenue of decline because only a moving boat is able to make waves!

By the Numbers

This issue of comfort is the principle driving force behind one of the questions that we ask churches in our Spiritual Awareness Survey.[1] It's a seemingly basic question, but it provides rather telling answers. The question says, "What kind of attitude do you have about this church?" We ask this because attitude plays an influential part in a person's worldview. The breakdown is as follows:

75.4% of those surveyed said that they have a positive attitude about their church.

23.2% of those surveyed said that they have mixed feelings about their church.

1.4% of those surveyed said that they have a negative attitude about their church.

The first possibility describes what we commonly see. Everyone is happy with the church. They're happy with the programs, the pastor, the worship services, and the fellowship. But the reason everyone's happy is because their needs are *always* met. We discovered through in-depth interviews that their happiness is a reflection that no one challenges them to move away from their comfort zones, or sacrifice their preferences for the benefit of others. They are never stretched. They never experience the discomfort of spiritual growing pains. The pastor is always available to them whenever needed. They're sheep that expect to be rubbed by the

FIGURE 2A
ATTITUDE PEOPLE HAVE TOWARD THEIR CHURCH

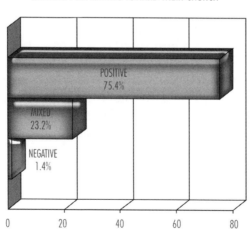

35

shepherd, and that's exactly what they get. It's *their* church, shepherded by someone to meet *their* needs, and that's how they like it. They may be encouraged to bring friends to Friendship Sundays, but that's the extent of the church's outreach. It's a comfortable, cocooned existence, and if anything threatens to interfere—such as changing the worship style, times or dates, parking away from the church for visitor accessibility, or phrasing church lingo in a way that visitors can understand, rumblings of discontent begin. While the positive attitudes may be prevalent, it's largely because the church is collectively looking through the wrong window.

The second possibility describes what the church should be. The church is organized around the purpose of making disciples. Its objective is to "turn people from pagans into missionaries" by the grace of God. The people are grounded in the word of God, urged to be missionaries in their neighborhoods and communities, and focused on carrying out God's will. They look through the biblical window of what it means to be the church. They understand that their needs will not always be met, but they consider the mission more important. They understand that sacrifice is a part of the plan. It's a church that is positive about its direction, leadership, and impact on the kingdom of God. That's the kind of church God can use. That's the kind of environment in which God moves. Attitudes are positive in this scenario because expectations are focused on kingdom results, not personal comfort issues. It is better to give than to always receive.

American Christians would be shocked to discover how Korean Christians are assimilated into ministry. There's no sign up board or pressure from the pastor to fill a vacant slot. Instead, they're thrown into ministry all the time. With little or no training, new Christians become instant ministers. On one of my visits to Korea, I was visiting with a pastor and a woman who had recently become a Christian. We encountered a man who was clearly possessed by an evil spirit. Guess which one of us cast out the demon? Not me. Not even the pastor. It was the new Christian! The pastor said, "Here, you do it!" He gave a forty-five second lesson and left the room, saying, "I'll be back in twenty minutes to see what God has done!" If you're a Christian in Korea, there's no such thing as a comfort zone.

Your Church: Wanted Dead or Alive?

I read a great illustration on the difference between live churches and dead churches. Which statement sounds like your church?

Live churches are constantly changing,
Dead churches don't have to.

Live churches have lots of noisy youth,
Dead churches are fairly quiet.

Live churches' expenses ALWAYS exceed their income,
Dead churches take in more than they ever dream of spending.

Live churches are intense and earnest about worship,
Dead churches aren't.

Live churches are filled with tithers,
Dead churches are filled with tippers.

Live churches dream great dreams for God,
Dead churches relive nightmares.

Live churches plan for the future,
Dead churches worship the past.

Live churches don't have "can't" in their vocabulary,
Dead churches have nothing but . . .

Live churches have fresh winds of love blowing . . .
Dead churches are full of bickering.[2]

Thomas à Kempis said, "If Christ is among us, then it is necessary that we sometimes yield up our own opinion . . . trust not too much to thine own opinion, but be ready also to hear the opinions of others." Your ability to sacrifice your comfort is one way to tell whether you're in a live or dead church.

The Posture of Sacrifice

Jesus, Paul, and many others in the New Testament continuously made sacrifices. It's a worldview that helps Christians avoid being tripped up by Satan's obstacles. In John Maxwell's book, *The 21 Irrefutable Laws Of Leadership,* he points out that one sacrifice is seldom going to be enough. "Sacrifice . . . is an ongoing process, not a one-time payment."[3]

The Window of Comfort models the mission. When your mission is to make disciples, you'll find yourself venturing into new territory on a continual basis. Life gets exciting! As John A. Shedd once declared, "A ship in harbor is safe—but that is not what ships are for." For a ship to fulfill its purpose, it has to leave the safe harbor! Reaching lost people will stretch you to leave your comfort zone. You'll grow and become all God has planned for you, and when you look through the Window of Comfort, you'll see a cross. And you'll rediscover your mission.

Lining up the Windows

Window 1:   Your Purpose Determines Your Mission
Window 2:   Your Comfort Determines Your Sacrifice

Getting a Better View

1. *Reflect on your own life and on sacrifice.* What does it mean to be a disciple? What were some of the sacrifices the disciples made in their lives? Have you ever experienced the connection between sacrifice and personal growth? Personal sacrifice and fulfillment?
2. *Organize a spiritual retreat with your friends, small group or family.* Design it around Philippians 2. Consider using

an outside facilitator. Spend time discussing the role of leadership. Are Christian leaders supposed to be concerned about not rocking the boat? Are you a people pleaser who might sacrifice God's goals so as not to offend others? What is the *role* of leadership? As a group, listen to my Church Doctor audiotape, *Attitude: The Difference That Makes A Difference.*

3. *Consider taking a short-term mission trip to another country.* Visit growing churches so you can see the sacrifices that Christians are making all over the world. Let God teach you to be missionary-minded. Focus on how effective mission work requires entering the culture of the unchurched—which is always uncomfortable for a missionary. If you need help organizing short-term mission trips, call Church Doctor Mission Trips at 1-800-626-8515.

4. *Get involved in a servant event.* If you have a family, do it together. Help rebuild areas that have been devastated by weather or go to where people are economically depressed and need help. Serve at a soup kitchen or a homeless shelter.

5. *Analyze the dollars your church spent over the last year.* Which are for members' comfort? Which are for ministry to others? Is there a balance? Which dollars—and what proportion—are spent on personal growth ministries that may stretch you, making you uncomfortable?

The Last Word

"When we started to see unchurched people come, the selfish, territorial attitudes of church people surprised me. But you have to decide what God has called you to do, not what the people want you to do."[4]

Michael Slaughter

Your Image Determines Your Impact

"If they want to come to our church, let them come—but we're not going to change our church for everybody."

Problems at Bible Fellowship

Bob and Mike were munching cookies and drinking coffee in the fellowship hall after worship one Sunday. The conversation began with happenings in the church, dipped through currents of sports, politics, lawn care, and eventually returned to the church. Bob blew on his coffee and asked, "Say, did you hear about what's going on down at St. Jude?"

"No. What are they up to now?"

"They're starting a worship service in Spanish for all those Hispanic people who have moved into the area."

Mike shook his head. "I'm sure glad we don't do that. I don't understand it. This is America. We speak English! I mean, if they want to worship in our churches, let 'em learn English. They're in *our* country after all. Don't you think?"

Meanwhile, in the basement, the church council of Bible Fellowship was embroiled in a hot debate about adding a new worship service. A group in the congregation wanted to begin a contemporary service. "It's a great way to keep the youth in a growing relationship with God," they said. But there was plenty of opposition. Margaret was quick to point out that to reduce the standard hymns to a bunch of modern "diddies" is dumbing down the worship service. It's an insult to God, and it undermines the *dignity* of worship. Margaret continued by saying that the pastor needed to start teaching the young people the *proper* way to worship—just like she was taught when she was a kid.

Following the debate on adding another worship service, the council received a proposal brought by the outreach team. It recommended spending approximately $10,000 over the next six months to advertise the church on some billboards in town and near heavily trafficked highways. Henry and Rita strongly objected.

"You want to spend $10,000 on billboards?" asked Henry. "You've gotta be kidding! What are we doing, joining Madison Avenue? Should we list our church right up there with Budweiser and Jack Daniels? Most of the people in this town know where our church is. Heck, they ought to—we've been here for 46 years! If they want to come, let them come! If you ask me, it's just a big waste of money to advertise something people already know about."

The council meeting ended, and as the members filed out, Margaret, Henry, and Rita met up with Bob and Mike. Margaret was still tense.

"Punk rock worship, that's all it is. Trying to please kids that don't respect their parents anyway. Guitars and drums inside our beautiful sanctuary—what a travesty!"

"Billboards!" Henry was muttering. "Whoever heard of advertising for people to come to church? Aren't people *supposed* to go to church? The whole town knows where we are. If they want to come, I'll welcome them with open arms. They're free to be here, so why act like a commercialized church?"

Henry and Rita looked at Margaret, Bob, and Mike. All were sadly shaking their heads.

"What has gotten into our church?"

Chew on this for a minute. Imagine yourself in the living room of heaven just before Jesus was born. The Father, Son, and Holy Spirit, are having a discussion. The Father declares that it's time to fulfill his promise. It's time to send Jesus to earth, and he begins to tell him what it's going to be like. He tells him that he's going to appear like a man. He's going to be born in a lowly stable—not a palace. He won't have the royalty that he has in heaven—he'll walk a humble path. He'll laugh, cry, suffer, and die. Many will disrespect him.

Now what would have happened if Jesus had an attitude like Margaret, Henry, and the others? Imagine if he had turned to the Father and said, "Father, why should I go to them? They've read all about us in the words of the prophets. They know where we are. You've been telling people about yourself for centuries! Let them come if they want to come."

Taking Your Church Public

The window through which you see your church's image determines the kind of impact your church can have in your community. Sometimes Christians feel others should come to them. That's a misunderstanding of what it means to be the church. It's religious chauvinism. The Great Commission strategy is to "go." In fact, the word "mission" means "to be sent." Jesus was sent to you, and now he sends you to the world. Yet, many people spend much of their time acting like others should come to them. Ads in the yellow pages, advertisements for fish fries and mailed brochures tend to put the responsibility on the people they're trying to reach. If that's all we do, it's not enough. The church should be aggressive by taking God's love in Christ to people. It's called, "going public."

But before you can take your Christianity public, you have to see your image through a biblical window. Walt Kallestad at Community Church of Joy in Phoenix, Arizona refers to the church as a "mission center."[1] That definition is based on a biblical worldview of the church. In a mission center, you're trained to take the gospel message *to* the world. The focus is outward, not inward. Churches that operate as mission centers develop ministries for the public, not just those inside the church. Their passion is for all people to share Christ's unfathomable love. Meeting needs and making disciples are what being a mission center is all about. It's all about going to others, on *their* level. It's grounded in the importance of going beyond the four walls of the building. It's what Jesus did. He met Zacchaeus as he balanced himself on the branch of a tree. The tree wasn't in the synagogue. Jesus was in the street! He forgave a woman caught in adultery. She wasn't a member of the church's women's group. Jesus met her "out there." He met the needs of the sick, lame, blind, dying, and hopeless. That was the emphasis behind his "public" ministry. His ministry was public because he took himself public to meet the needs of those he was trying to reach. Walt Kallestad says in his book, *Entertainment Evangelism*, "The church needs to be even friendlier than Disneyland."[2] Jesus went the distance. Are you willing to be a missionary? Is your church willing to become a mission center? Is it a body reaching out with Christ's love, or is it just a building with a sign announcing worship times? It's an important question to ask because your image determines what kind of impact you can have in your community.

Helping Others See Jesus

Let's go back again to Zacchaeus. What was his problem? It wasn't being small. That was how God created him. His problem was that he wanted to see Jesus and *people were in the way*. They weren't necessarily bad people. Like Margaret, Henry, and the others at Bible Fellowship, they were doing their religious thing. They were also there to see Jesus. They weren't purposely blocking Zacchaeus from Jesus. Inadvertently, they had gotten in Zacchaeus' way, and he couldn't connect to Jesus. You know the rest of the story—he climbed a tree, and Jesus went to him. Later that day Jesus went to his house, and salvation came to Zacchaeus.

Think back to the problems at Bible Fellowship. Bob and Mike were dumbfounded that St. Jude was starting services in Spanish to attract Hispanics. Mike objected on the grounds that because they're in the United States, they needed to learn English in order to worship. Is that a willingness to meet people where they are? What kind of image was St. Jude

Church concerned with—one that embodied a mission center, or one that adhered to language preferences?

Or what about Margaret? To her, starting a contemporary service for the youth meant giving in to popular demand. It wasn't true to how she was taught as a kid. She was less concerned about meeting the spiritual needs of the youth and more concerned about maintaining her own opinion of tradition—her own wants and needs. She was looking at her church's image through an unbiblical window. Therefore, her perceptions of how the church should respond to needs were distorted. She saw the church making an impact by teaching others how to worship "properly," like when she was a kid. Her worldview of church wasn't a mission center. This window means doing what's necessary to be effective, to get God's love in Jesus Christ through to people. It means following Paul's example in 1 Corinthians 9:22 when he says, "I have become all things to all people, that I might by all means save some."

Or what about the uproar over spending money on billboards? The outreach committee recommended advertising on billboards. Those opposed to the idea couldn't understand the rationale behind the suggestion. The disagreement occurred because of conflicting worldviews. Henry and Rita had a worldview of the church that had little to do with outreach. In their opinion, people were free to come, but the church had no responsibility to go public. They were firmly entrenched in a "y'all come" attitude. In all three examples, they were doing their religious thing, but they were also getting in the way of those who need to see Jesus.

You should take the gospel to the marketplace—not expect others to cross the stained glass barrier. During Jesus' public ministry, the Pharisees never understood this important window. The Pharisees and teachers of the law were mortified that Jesus sat down and ate with tax collectors and other outcasts in society. It just wasn't how things were done. Why be a teacher if it means hanging around with the unkempt, the sinful, and the poor? Why surround yourself with people who don't observe religious customs, feasts, dates, or laws? Why go to them when all they have to do is come to you? In turn, the Pharisees would hang around the synagogue and wait for people to come. What kind of people? The *right* people, *good* people, *clean* people, people like *them*.

Why was Jesus effective in reaching people? He met them where they were. He met them where they were hurting. He healed them where they were bleeding and suffering. He touched them where God had broken them and showed them their sinfulness. He saw them at their dirtiest and in their least likable states, and communicated that he loved them more than anything in the world. He accepted them the way they were. He spoke the language they understood. The people he was trying to reach were drawn to him because he went to them! Jesus didn't behave like the Pharisees because he looked through a mission window. As a result, Jesus was incredibly effective at doing what he wanted to do most: change lives for eternity. The Pharisees didn't reach out to people in their state of need—on the contrary—Jesus accused them of increasing burdens. "They tie up heavy burdens, hard to bear, and lay them on the shoulders of others; but they themselves are unwilling to lift a finger to move them" (Matthew 23:4). By contrast, Jesus said, "Come to me, all you that are weary and are carrying heavy burdens, and I will give you rest" (Matthew 11:28). The Pharisees had an image (worldview) that deterred people from God. Jesus encouraged people to come before God in all their sinfulness and be cleansed. To multiply himself, he sent his disciples out to the world. In Luke 10 he sends out seventy-two of them, saying, "The harvest is plentiful, but the laborers are few; therefore ask the Lord of the harvest to send out laborers into his harvest. Go on your way. See, I am sending you out like lambs into the midst of wolves" (Luke 10:2-3). Jesus wasn't setting up shop for people to come see him—he was starting a movement!

In which camp would you place yourself? Which window reflects your church?

By the Numbers

Inviting someone to your church is a basic form of outreach. Though it requires some preparation and follow-up if the invitation is accepted, it's a comfortable form of outreach for many because it involves bringing people to their turf.

Our Mission Awareness survey asks members a question that pertains to how often they invite people to church. Of the people we surveyed, only 24.5% indicated that they had invited someone in the last month. Another 43.8% said they had in the last year, and 31.7% said they hadn't invited anyone to their church in over one year.

If inviting someone to church causes the least amount of personal discomfort, why do only one in four active Christians do it only monthly? Part of the explanation lies in

FIGURE 3A
HOW OFTEN CHRISTIANS INVITE OTHERS TO CHURCH

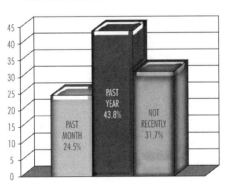

Henry's answer for not wanting to advertise on billboards. Many Christians believe that if their church is visible, they have no responsibility for whether or not visitors attend. But Jesus doesn't intend for you to be reactive. George Barna writes, "By refining the thinking of Christians so that they see themselves as 24-hour-a-day marketing agents for the Church, we can start to make the Church a more personal place . . . In an environment in which people are actively searching for institutions which promote a focus on people and the satisfaction of felt needs, we can make significant headway in improving the image of the local body."[3] To have maximum impact, your church needs to be proactive—a living organism—as opposed to a dusty institution.

Marketplace Christianity: the Use of Enterprise Ministries

Churches in the near future will look different. Some will look more like malls, with the different "stores" representing various ministries, and the anchor "store" being the worship center. It will be an effective way to "go" to the community because marketplace ministry combines cultural relevance with meaningful, God-centered service and outreach.

Other areas in the church would house "enterprise ministries." These are designed to connect people with the church in ways that meet needs, provide services, and establish relationships through which the gospel is shared. Some of these enterprise ministries have been a part of church life for years: preschools, daycare centers, spaghetti suppers, and fish fries. The primary objective is to "create a unique environment to attract and nurture a community of believers whose spiritual-growth needs may not have been met in traditional church settings. A key concept is to present the 'church experience' in a way that relates to people's lives,"[4] says church architect David Price.

The opportunity for you to reach your community through new enterprise ministries are expanding every day. Enterprise ministries begin, mentally, with others, not ourselves. Instead of dank, neglected libraries, some churches are providing bookstores patterned after companies like Barnes and Noble. People from the community can enjoy hot beverages while perusing materials that can help them grow. Teen nightclubs are making their way onto church campuses.

These provide Christian teens with a place to socialize, hear music that speaks to them, invite non-believers, and sponsor concerts by Christian artists—all in a responsible and safe setting. What else is on the horizon? Here are a few examples of other enterprise ministries that I've seen across the country: mortuaries, wedding chapels, full service restaurants, "airplane safe" (edited for general audiences) video stores, counseling centers, retirement villages, retreat centers, leadership training centers, and Bible college extensions. One church in Phoenix, Arizona was told by city planners that they had to provide a large retention pond. They saw it as an opportunity to provide a water park! All of these enterprise ministries are designed to support the image of the church as a mission center; engaging people and sharing Christ. Marketplace ministry goes to the people instead of depending on them to "come to church." It is a worldview that church is for others, not just for self. This healthy image has a tremendous impact.

Not Without Risks

Not all of the above ministries will work everywhere. Teen nightclubs won't thrive in areas heavily populated by senior citizens, and retirement villages won't meet many needs near a college campus. All of these enterprise ministries are organized to meet needs in the community. That's what going public with your church is all about! It's a deliberate effort to find out what the needs are, see what God is doing, and then start ministries that speak to those needs. It's the Jesus approach—and it works! People are going to discover much more about your faith when you listen to them.

Keep in mind, however, that there are challenges and dangers to such ministries. Most apparent is what might be described as *"fat grams without soul food"*—providing the ministry, but minimizing the main purpose of sharing the gospel and making disciples. Unfortunately, it happens all the time. Numerous church preschools are superior at providing a safe atmosphere that prepares children for kindergarten, but presenting the gospel to the parents gets buried on the priority list. When this pattern is repeated, the church can become similar to the modern day YMCA—a Christian mission idea that has turned into a community gymnasium. Today we often find church owned family life centers with no program of ministry and fish fries with no evangelistic purpose. So if you help start enterprise ministries, you'll need to focus on an intentional mission to clearly communicate what business you're in. As creative and exciting as some of these enterprise ministries are, it is important to understand that these ministries are a means—not the end. They're creative platforms for outreach. Unless people are led to a relationship with Jesus Christ, assimilated into the family of the church, and equipped for the ongoing discipleship, the enterprise ministry will fall short of its incredible potential.

Through which window do you see your image? Will you be content with opening the church doors on Sunday and welcoming anyone who comes, or will you be a mission center reaching out to people in search of a Savior? Seeing your image through the eyes of Jesus definitely determines your impact on your community—and on eternity!

Lining up the Windows

Window 1:   Your Purpose Determines Your Mission
Window 2:   Your Comfort Determines Your Sacrifice
Window 3:   Your Image Determines Your Impact

Getting a Better View

1. Examine your approach to affecting your community. What percent of your church's ministry requires your community to come to you? (Not just "come" physically, but mentally, emotionally, culturally, and socially?) Publish these results in a newsletter or bulletin and challenge people to brainstorm ways you can reach people. Has your church designed a strategic plan for outreach? If not, the Church Doctor consultation ministry can help you develop a three-year plan for missions.

2. *If you haven't done so already, start a small group ministry in your home.* Build it with a strong outreach foundation. Invite unchurched friends, relatives, and acquaintances from work or school to visit. In this way, you will be reaching people you know, but touching them on neutral turf. Get trained through a lifestyle evangelism training program like *Heart To Heart: Sharing Christ With a Friend* (available from the Church Doctor Ministries).

3. *Organize a second Vacation Bible School away from your church campus.* Hold it in a park or rent space in a mall. Don't say "it's difficult enough trying to get help for one VBS, let alone another." Some people may volunteer for this simply because it's a cutting edge outreach event.

4. *Start a business Bible luncheon.* Encourage members and seekers to meet weekly for a Bible Study during lunch hour. Hold it in a central location near a group of businesses and be sure to be respectful of their time!

5. *If your church holds an annual Easter pageant or Christmas production, consider having it somewhere other than your church.* Rent the local civic center, or a theater. People will consider it to be neutral ground, and enjoy the production. Follow it up with future outreach events away from your church's campus.

The Last Word

"Rescuing people in spiritual peril frequently requires us to strategically venture into their environment."[5]

Lee Strobel

Your Desires Determine Your Priorities

"I don't know what the Bible says, but I think our church should do more for the members."

Taking the Ball and Going Home

I was consulting a church in Northern Michigan. On the second day, I was having lunch and interviewing a group of adults who led the youth. The conversation was touching upon some of the God-sized visions their church was pursuing when a woman named Marilyn blurted out, "I personally want us to go back to one worship service. Ever since we went to two worship services, I don't get to see everybody. I really want our church to feel more like a family again. That was what I liked about it for so long. I'm so unhappy about it that I've considered leaving the church, and finding a smaller one!" Since she was scheduled for an individual interview later in the day, I asked if we could wait until then to discuss her concern. But all day I was bothered by her comments. Marilyn reminded me of a childhood friend of mine who saw things through that same window. His name was Tommy. He used to come over and we'd usually spend the afternoons playing basketball. But he always wanted to play his game, his way, and by his rules. Whenever I suggested a rule change, or disputed a call, Tommy would literally take his ball and go home. What Marilyn was telling me that day was that if she didn't get her way in the church, she, too, would take her ball and go home.

At another church I consulted, there was a dispute over what God was leading them to do in their area of the city. In their literature they proudly described themselves as an inner city church, but after spending five minutes inside the building, I knew better. First of all, the building itself was well over one hundred years old. The architecture was ornate, with a prominent steeple, majestic stonework, and stained glass mosaics. It was beautiful—breathtaking—but also completely unrelated to this century. There were few adequate places to accommodate multimedia presentations. The church had never installed air conditioning, and the summer humidity was treacherous. Although the church building was one of a kind in aesthetics, it was culturally relevant only to people who lived before televisions, cell phones, and the Internet. Few people from the inner city were visiting. Those who visited rarely returned. The only way this church was ever going to effectively speak to the people they were supposedly trying to reach would be to tear down the sanctuary and build a more indigenous and culturally-sensitive worship center. Astonished, they pointed at the regal setting and wondered how I could ever make such a recommendation. I asked them, "Don't you think that reaching the people in your area is what God wants?"

Exasperated, they replied, "Well, yes! Of course!"

"Don't you think that God wants you to do that in the most effective way possible?"

"Yes! But we don't want to do it if it means tearing down the sanctuary!"

In a nutshell, that was the problem. What God could accomplish was coming into conflict with what they wanted, and until they saw their priorities through a biblical window, their preferences would prevail. In effect, looking through a biblical window changes your desires to God's priorities.

The Power of Priorities

Earlier I stated that how you see your comfort ultimately determines your posture of sacrifice. Jesus never put his comfort above his mission. Therefore, the sacrifices he made were based on accomplishing that mission. In the same way, how you see your desires ultimately determines your priorities. In the church, there is a tendency for Christians to place their will above God's will, their priorities above God's.

The problem is that God never says that it's okay to place what we want over what he wants! For the church to be what the church should be, we have to understand it the way he does. Many churches pray the Lord's Prayer during worship services. Everyone prays "*your* will be done." Then, after the worship service, many of those same people file into congregational meetings and demand what *they* want. Analyzing our priorities through a biblical window requires purposefully seeking and knowing God's will. It means subordinating our own desires to God's, and operating the church accordingly. It means changing the tone of congregational meetings from votes to prayers, and from politicking to get your own way to hungering to find God's way.

Controlling Maintenance, Capturing Mission

If the church is ever going to seriously pursue world evangelization, it can't let *maintenance* overtake *mission*. In my book *Move Your Church To Action*, I define maintenance as anything that focuses on maintaining the institution.[1] Every church needs to have some maintenance. Walls need to be painted, facilities require periodic updates, bills need to paid, and the grass has to be cut. But when maintenance becomes a higher priority than fulfilling God's mission, the church is lopsided. Jose Ortega y Gasset said, "There are people who so arrange their lives that they feed themselves only on the side dishes." Maintenance consists of the side dishes, while making disciples is the main course! There has to be a balance, and that balance comes from praying, listening, and paying close attention to what God is doing. This balance doesn't necessarily mean a fifty/fifty proposition, but rather an understanding of how the two can be syncopated—with God's desire taking top priority.

The apostles, in the book of Acts, demonstrated this kind of balance. In Acts 6, they recognized that a large chunk of their time was spent caring for widows and performing maintenance obligations. They knew that wasn't God's desire for them at all, and their God-inspired mission-mindedness led them to commission several others to assume those responsibilities. Caring for the widows wasn't wrong, but it was hindering the spread of the gospel.

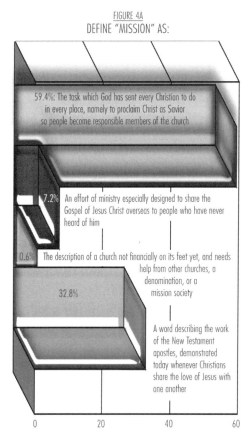

FIGURE 4A
DEFINE "MISSION" AS:

59.4%: The task which God has sent every Christian to do in every place, namely to proclaim Christ as Savior so people become responsible members of the church

7.2% An effort of ministry especially designed to share the Gospel of Jesus Christ overseas to people who have never heard of him

0.6% The description of a church not financially on its feet yet, and needs help from other churches, a denomination, or a mission society

32.8%

A word describing the work of the New Testament apostles, demonstrated today whenever Christians share the love of Jesus with one another

0   20   40   60

By the Numbers

Churches aren't supposed to be maintenance-oriented institutions simply preserving the status quo. How do you change yours? The answer lies in understanding how God defines mission. How do you define mission? Our Mission Awareness Survey asks this question, and the results are similar to the responses from a previous question about the main purpose of the church.

Remember, "mission" means "to be sent." But it isn't confined to a specific territory overseas. America is the third largest mission field in the world. Do you realize that the mission field is here as well as anywhere else people live who don't know Christ as their Savior? Answer D received the second largest amount of responses, which further indicates that one third of regularly church-going Christians are caught up in the belief that sharing God's love *with each other* (other Christians) is the highest priority. This is why many focus on maintaining the comfortable institution more than operating the church as a mission center. It's also a primary reason why 80% of churches in the United States are plateaued or declining. There is a significant problem in the way churches balance maintenance and mission, and it stems from having unbiblical priorities.

Many church committees and boards are maintenance oriented. They are designed to address certain areas that need upkeep in the church. A Board of Trustees may be responsible to make repairs around the building, or a Banner Committee may get together to sew banners for the sanctuary. Those groups are maintenance-oriented, but they serve a valuable purpose within the church. There are many other committees that function the same way. But many meeting agendas, pastors' calendars, activity schedules, fundraisers, and budgets are also steered toward maintaining the institution, whether it be the building or the needs of the members. The scales tip heavily toward preserving the church, not being sent to the world. Charles Van Engen said, "John 3:16 doesn't say that God so loved the church that he gave his only begotten Son. It says that God so loved the world that he gave his only begotten Son. Our mission is the world, not the church."

We prioritize what we want over what God wants. Many times, when a church begins a new worship service, it will often survey its own people and overlook getting information from the unchurched people in the community as well. They seek, internally, what times they would be most likely to attend, what style of worship speaks to them, what style of dress they prefer, etc. It stems from looking through our own window of desire rather than what God wants.

Harvest Priorities

John 4 illustrates what I call "Harvest Priorities." Most Christians are familiar with the story of Jesus and the woman at the well, but I find that some of the most important principles are uncovered *after* verse 26. Prior to this point, Jesus had spoken to a Samaritan woman (a cultural taboo), about living water, her sinful life, and her encounter with the Messiah. This one, short conversation with Jesus radically changed her worldview. Soon after this, Jesus' disciples returned from town. Remember, this was pre-Pentecost—the church didn't fully exist yet. The disciples were the embryonic form of the church. When they returned, they were surprised to see Jesus talking to the woman, but they didn't say anything. You can almost hear their conversation drying up as they stumble upon Jesus talking to this Samaritan woman. No one asked, "What do *you* want?" Or, "Why are you talking with *her*?" Two different worldviews were at work. The disciples didn't understand what their leader was doing, and didn't have the guts to ask him. They were viewing the situation through the wrong window. They were seeing an intruder.

Verse 28 says that the woman *left her water jar* and went back to town. It's a passage that often goes unnoticed, but it reveals the kind of amazing transformation that only Jesus can make. The Samaritan woman's priorities were dramatically changed. She came to the well for water, but she left without even taking her water jars back with her. She came for what she wanted, and left doing what God wanted. Her window would be changed forever. She instantly became a missionary to her people, with a desire to share Jesus. In verse 29 she exclaimed, "Come and see a man who told me everything I have ever done. He cannot be the Messiah, can he?" (John 4:29). Her desire had been transformed from maintenance, which impacted her priority (taking care of her need for water), to the desire for mission (which led to the priority of telling her whole town, "This guy could be the Messiah"). Her whole world was completely changed. Now, her priority was getting the message to Samaria.

> **The woman at the well came to the well for what she wanted, and left doing what God wanted.**

Meanwhile, the disciples were on a different plane. In verse 31, they say "Rabbi, eat something." They didn't ask him about his conversation with the woman. Nor did they inquire as to why she suddenly darted off without her water jars. Instead, they focused on their top desire. What was important to them? Their stomachs! Jesus was doing missionary work—he had empowered the Samaritan woman and changed her life. The disciples were more concerned about having a potluck! In verse 32, Jesus began reshaping their worldview by saying, "I have food to eat that you do not know about." He had a mission, but he knew their priorities. He used the word "food" because they were talking about food, but he was trying to turn their attention to the bigger picture—the biblical window. He was pointing out that something more important than food and water was going on. Jesus didn't feed himself on the side dishes; his appetite was for the main course!

But the disciples' worldviews didn't change quite that fast. They were still looking through the wrong window. They mumbled among themselves, "Surely no one has brought him something to eat?" (John 4:33) They wanted to eat and have fellowship, but Jesus was focused on the mission. He says, "My food is to do the will of him who sent me and to complete his work" (John 4:34). Jesus had harvest priorities, and his desire was to obey his Father. His staple diet consisted of doing the will of the Father and finishing his work. The Father's desires fashioned his priorities.

How about your priorities? As Jesus has changed your life, are you more concerned about a potluck? Or is your "food" doing the will of God and finishing his work? Are you on the main course of God's mission to the world, or are you repeatedly caught in maintenance side dishes? Spend some time praying about this. It may reveal some of your priorities that you won't like, but God is all about changing worldviews. He wants his desires to be your desires, and his priorities to be your priorities. If you and your church see the world from his perspective, you'll never be out of balance.

Lining up the Windows

Window 1:   Your Purpose Determines Your Mission
Window 2:   Your Comfort Determines Your Sacrifice
Window 3:   Your Image Determines Your Impact
Window 4:   Your Desires Determine Your Priorities

Getting a Better View

1. A strong personal devotional life is key for following God's plan for your life. Is your devotional life on the upswing, or on a downslide? Schedule ample time for Bible study, prayer, and reaching out to people who don't know Christ.

2. How well does your church balance maintenance and mission? Where does your church's money, time, and resources go? How much effort is spent maintaining the institution instead of invigorating the mission? Hire an outside consultant to assess your congregation's balance.

3. How does your church select its leaders? By a vote? By default when no one else wants the job? Select the leaders at your church from those who attend a regularly scheduled Bible study. Make sure they know the desires of God, and have shown that they subordinate their preferences to Christ's priorities. Getting to know God and what he wants comes from studying his only blueprint—the Bible. How can you discern God's will if you aren't studying his blueprint?

4. If your church is heavy on the maintenance side, evaluate your outreach programs. How does your church speak to those who don't know Christ? Think back to the last chapter. Does your church actively take itself into the community? Are your members trained in lifestyle evangelism?

5. Purchase Heart To Heart – Sharing Christ with a Friend, *available from Church Doctor Ministries. Heart To Heart* is a valuable tool that can help you learn lifestyle evangelism. Every Christian has a mission, and the proper training combined with boldness inspired by the Holy Spirit can spark an outreach blaze in your life.

The Last Word

A man walked into the pastor's office and said: "I want to join the church. But don't ask me to do anything. I don't want any part of any organization. I don't want to do any work. I'll come to church when I feel like it, but that's it." The pastor replied: "I see. Well, you're at the wrong address. Here, go to this address just down the road. They have exactly what you want." The man left and went down the street until he came to the address which the pastor gave him, and was shocked to find himself at the entrance to a cemetery.

Faith takes action.

Vic Halboth

Your Blessings Determine Your Giving

"I don't think it's anybody's business what I give to the church!"

God Loves a Cheerful Giver

The father wanted to help his son learn an important lesson in stewardship. So one Sunday he gave him a quarter and a dollar bill for the offering plate and told him to contribute whatever he felt was right. Whatever he didn't give, he could keep. When the boy returned, his father asked, "Well, son, how much did you give?"

The boy said, "Well, I was going to give the dollar, but before they passed the plate, the minister announced "The Lord loves a cheerful giver. I knew I'd be more cheerful if I gave the quarter and kept the dollar, so I did!"

This chapter is on the issue of financial stewardship, and how you can see it through a biblical window. Many pastors pride themselves on how rarely they preach about money. But money is a frequent topic in the Bible. The absence of a biblical approach encourages a false belief system about finances. Some Christians are tippers instead of givers. Some pastors wait until a crisis hits before teaching about giving, and even then, some go about it from the wrong perspective—like Pastor Johnson.

Give to the Church?

Pastor Johnson took a deep breath, silently asked God for courage, and leaning over his pulpit, addressed his congregation. "I don't preach very often about money, but God calls us to be good managers of our resources. Our church is facing a significant challenge. Right now we're about $12,000 behind budget. Now, I know you people love the Lord and care for this church, so I felt that I should let you know. The elders and I have crunched the numbers, and we've concurred that if each of us gives an extra $200.00 to the church within the next month, we'll meet the budget."

With that plea, Pastor Johnson has just reinforced an unbiblical worldview about Christian financial stewardship. He issued a challenge for his congregation to give an amount of $200.00 each to the church. On the surface, that might sound innocent enough, but there are two unbiblical flaws in Pastor Johnson's request. First, Scripture doesn't focus on giving an amount, but a percentage. Giving back to God should be done in a proportionate way, instead of asking for a set amount, like $200.00. Second, giving *to* the church also indicates an unbiblical worldview. God doesn't ask his people to give to the church. He doesn't say that the motive *or the amount* of what someone gives should be formulated by the purpose or the cause. Budgets, fundraisers, or pleas shouldn't be catalysts for giving. God does say to give back *from* what he has given. It's always returning from God's blessings. So, as Pastor Johnson preached about giving a *dollar amount to the church*, he preached an unbiblical stewardship worldview on two levels!

Michelle met Roberta for a cup of coffee. After a few moments of small talk, Michelle finally got up the courage to ask Roberta a question she'd wanted to ask for a long time. "Roberta, how much do you and Hal give to church?"

Roberta responded, "Well, we give about $25 per week—when we're there."

"How did you arrive at that amount?" asked Michelle.

"Well, I'll have to think about that . . . " replied Roberta. "I think . . . I really don't know. It's what we gave last year . . . and the year before that . . . it's what we've given for as long as I can remember."

Looking through the biblical window, the way you see your blessings determines your giving. Proportionate giving is one of the keys to having the resources for an effective church. As God gives more, the amount will grow, even though the percentage or proportion might stay the same. We work with many churches that are far below their financial potential. Loren Meade of the Alban Institute says that finances are the Achilles' Heel of the 21st century. As we dig deeper, we find that they aren't really facing a resource challenge, but a giving challenge. They've never learned to operate through the biblical window that directs Christians to give back to God from what he's given them! When there's a clear understanding of proportionate giving, churches, regardless of their socio-economic status, have all the resources they need to do God's work. You can't outgive God!

By the Numbers

Why do so many Christians think first of an amount of money to give to the work of the Lord through their church? The biblical window is to give by percentage. Through our research, we have tried to understand the stewardship worldviews prevalent among Christians. Our research has uncovered startling statistics about financial giving patterns.

FIGURE 5A
PERCENTAGE GIVING AMONG THOSE WE SURVEYED

Proportionate giving is the practice of giving a dedicated percentage of your gross income to the Lord's work through the church. It's given before taxes, groceries, gasoline, etc. This biblical window comes from 1 Corinthians 16:2, which says, "On the first day of every week, each of you is to put aside and save whatever extra you earn, . . . " Leviticus 27:30 also says, "All tithes from the land . . . are the Lord's; they are holy to the Lord." It was common in the Old Testament to give 10% as a minimum. In the New Testament, that concept was accepted and exceeded. It wasn't a law, just a practice—an understanding that a portion of what God had given would be given back.

According to our research, only about one fourth of active Christians give ten percent or more of their income to the Lord's work through their church. The implications for what the church can and can't do are enormous! R.T. Kendall said, "Tithing is the solution no one talks about . . . If every Christian tithed, every congregation would be free of financial worries and could begin truly to be the salt of the earth. If every Christian would tithe, the church would begin to make an impact on the world that would change it. The church instead is paralyzed."[1]

Finances are God's fuel for the engine of ministry, yet so many churches are hamstrung by a lack of financial support. What is truly disturbing is that our research shows almost one in three people indicated that they give 4% or less! No wonder many churches are financially dry!

Aside from the fact that this method of giving doesn't work and prohibits churches from fully functioning the way God intended, it also ignores God's wonderful promise regarding giving back to him. Through the prophet Malachi, God rebuked the descendants of Jacob for holding back from God. "Will anyone rob God? Yet you are robbing me! But you say, 'How are we robbing you?' In your tithes and offerings! You are cursed with a curse, for you are robbing me—the whole nation of you!" (Malachi 3:8-9). Then he gives this wonderful promise, "'Bring the whole tithe into the storehouse, that there my be food in my house. Test me in this,' says the Lord Almighty, and see if I will not throw open the floodgates of heaven and pour out so much blessing that you will not have room enough for it.'" (verse 10 NIV).

It's a thrill to be in God's biblical window of giving, experience the blessings, share those blessings in ministry, and be a blessing to others. I can't think of anyone who would want to rob God, can you? Not only has he provided forgiveness for sin, but he's also promised to see that all my needs for living are taken care of.

Giving a set amount works well from an institutional and managerial point of view. The church knows how much money to expect, and then it can plan the budget accordingly. It's the safe and human way. But the divine and faithful way is to teach people to give proportionately. For many, this is a different window for understanding how God sees finances. It stretches you to move beyond planning your church's work by the budget. It stimulates planning by faith in response to blessings. When this happens, the church moves from being a managed institution to a divine enterprise. Rather than emphasizing giving by an amount, it focuses on a percentage. J. Oswald Sanders said, "The basic question is not how much of our money we should give to God, but how much of God's money we should keep for ourselves." If you don't understand proportionate giving, maybe you shouldn't be on your church's leadership board—because you'll make decisions *based on your worldview*. If you aren't looking at your or the church's finances through a biblical window, you might not see with faith the journey God has given you.

Godly stewardship doesn't involve giving to the church to provide a budget, but giving from the blessings that God has given to the Lord's work. One of the many differences in the biblical window is that percentage giving increases the amount of offering as people experience prosperity and the blessings of God. That means that over time, as people experience growth and prosperity, so does God's work through their church. No matter what the level of income, the percentage stays the same. If the income decreases, the amount given may decrease—but the percentage is constant. God doesn't require equal giving. But he challenges his people for equal sacrifice. As trust in God to provide increases, God may lead the individual to raise that percentage. There's a misconception that wealthy people automatically "carry the financial weight" of the rest of the congregation. But stewardship author Waldo Werning puts it this way, "Better incomes never have, and never will produce better givers. Faith determines what we will give: The stronger the faith, the higher the percentage; the weaker the faith, the lower the percentage. Our prayer should be, 'Lord, increase my faith,' not, 'Lord, increase my income so I can give more.'"[2] I was talking with a wealthy Christian once who told me, "It's not that I can't give any more—it's that doing so would be unhealthy for my church. They think because I have all this money that they can sit on the bench and not have to give back to God." He had it right. His faith was strong, and his stewardship was sound, but his congregation felt he should carry the weight. Your congregation can have financial vitality, with everyone playing an important part, through proportionate giving. It's an entire reversal of the way most Christians approach the concept of giving. It is a biblical approach that releases abundant blessings for the work of the kingdom. This, in turn, empowers your church to be the healthy, vital, and productive ministry that God has intended it to be.

Kingdom Investing

Giving according to an amount can drive home the unhealthy impression that offerings are given to keep the church running. If Christians believe that they simply "give to the church," then they fall into a belief pattern where as long as the church doors are open and the staff is paid, everything is fine. But what if Christians viewed their finances from an investment perspective? On these two separate sides, you can see the difference between a maintenance oriented mindset and a mission oriented mindset. Churches need to be able to identify the corporate wealth of the church as 10% or more, and no less. A key factor in this is the role of leadership in discussing financial empowerment.

Pastors should teach biblical stewardship often, and challenge Christians to trust God's plan. Pastors also need to be trained to help wealthy people in the spiritual management of giving generously from what God has given them. This doesn't mean picking their pockets, or taking from them—that is not financial development from the biblical window. By approaching wealthy people about financial giving, pastors help them understand that as God has been rich to them, they need to be rich toward God. As Larry Burkett puts it, in " . . . abundance, the normal tendency is to feel secure and less involved . . . dangers of abundance are much more subtle than those of poverty."[3]

Many wealthy people are what I call "big picture" thinkers. They are entrepreneurial people who see beyond the immediate. When they are encouraged to look through the biblical window of stewardship, they become excited about ministry beyond the local church—ministry on a much bigger scale. They can find great fulfillment by releasing wealth to make a big difference on a grand scale.

In Luke 12 we see what can happen when wealthy people are not generous toward God. Jesus teaches this lesson in the parable of the rich fool. In the parable, a rich man looks over his plentiful crop, and decides that the time has come to sit back and take life easy. He had accumulated enough to warrant retirement. Do you look at life that way sometimes? Secularized media is constantly trying to convince you that the best math is: the more you accumulate, the happier you'll be. But Jesus says in the same night the rich fool declared his retirement, God took his life from him. He ends by saying, "This is how it will be with anyone who stores up things for himself but is not rich toward God" (Luke 12:21). I've known wealthy people who were taught God's principles for stew-

ardship for the very first time because they were challenged
to explore God's blueprint for financial stewardship. It completely changed their whole worldview on giving. As a result,
quite a few of those people began second careers in the
ministry, in parachurch organizations, as missionaries, and
as empowering donors. How you see your blessings determines your giving. How you give impacts your blessings, too!

You also need to help others think beyond your church.
God's work is so much bigger than that! Many missionaries
and parachurch ministries are in need of resources. World
evangelization provides opportunities for financial support
in many areas beyond the local church. You can build into
the lives of missionaries by offering personalized missionary
support. Not only can you provide financial leverage, you
can also learn more about the mission field, offer prayers for
the family, and offer a place for them to stay while they're
home on furlough.

Finances should never be given blindly. While it is our
privilege and honor to give back to God from what he's given,
you should help your church, mission team, or parachurch
ministry focus clearly on those goals they want to accomplish. An article in *Time* magazine indicated that as many
young billionaires are inventing a new age of philanthropy,
they have a high demand for accountability. You should give,
but you also need to keep ministry leaders accountable for
using the money for productive efforts.

Kingdom investing also includes what Lyle Schaller has
termed, "left pocket" and "right pocket wealth." The right
pocket wealth reflects your *income*. The biblical model calls
for faith to return a minimum of 10% of this pocket to the
Lord for his work. The left pocket represents *accumulated
wealth*. When someone receives an inheritance, sells stock or
property, receives a gift, or receives other unexpected blessings, that is left pocket wealth. In the case of selling stock, it's
money that you didn't even work for—it worked for you!
Giving back to God from both the left and right pockets can
enable your church to minister to more people, meet more

needs, and share the Gospel with more people in more countries.

Giving back to God from what He's given you is a privilege and an honor, not a duty. Everything in the world belongs to God anyway—a gift for us to manage. He gives freely, but gives us the privilege of partnership—to invest in His work in the world. This revolutionizes what may seem like a joyless duty, and turns it into an exciting investment in God's eternal enterprise. How you see your blessings really does determine your giving.

Lining up the Windows

Window 1:   Your Purpose Determines Your Mission
Window 2:   Your Comfort Determines Your Sacrifice
Window 3:   Your Image Determines Your Impact
Window 4:   Your Desires Determine Your Priorities
Window 5:   Your Blessings Determine Your Giving

Getting a Better View

1. Learn all you can about stewardship. Make sure the focus is on percentage giving. Understand that you're giving *from* what God has blessed you, not *to* the church. Practice first fruits giving, off the top. Enjoy joyful giving. Sponsor a Kingdom Investing Clinic at your church.[4]

2. Change your yearly pledge to a percentage commitment. Encourage others to take God up on His promise to provide for all their needs. Take the challenge to raise your giving by one percent per year. Reflect each year whether it makes any difference as God meets your needs.

3. Analyze the giving of others in your church by using an anonymous questionnaire to discern the percentage of income giving levels. Monitor this each year and see if the aggregate total is changing in the right direction for your church.

4. Change the name "budget" to an "administrative spending guide," and use it only among administrative leadership. Put the rest of your energy into teaching the biblical window of stewardship. Teach left and right pocket wealth.

5. Cultivate your "big picture" thinkers. They're people who give plenty to the church, but they also think beyond the local church. With a strong sense of security, put them in touch with big picture counselors. They can help them see where they can make an impact on the world for the Kingdom. They will be fulfilled and your church will benefit from their activity beyond.

The Last Word

"Stewardship and generosity are where the rubber meets the road in our lifestyle as Christians."[5]

Stephen A. Macchia

Your Abundance Determines Your Possibilities

"Before we get too excited about this project, Pastor, I want to know, how much is this going to cost?"

The Big Question

The last chapter focused on the window of giving. This one is on the window of spending, and how you look at it.

Bob addressed the congregational meeting. It was an exciting day for him because his committee had studied, reviewed, and prepared to present what they perceived to be an outstanding program that would help their congregation reach unchurched people in their community.

"We have a new evangelism program that we've been evaluating for seven months. Several of us have attended training seminars at the church that developed it. We've also interviewed other churches that have used this program effectively. We're very impressed and excited. But before I get into the details and call on those who have been a part of this research, I'm wondering if there are any initial questions."

As Harold stood up to speak, the room fell silent. Bob winced. His blood pressure soared. He immediately wished he hadn't offered an impromptu Q&A session.

"Yeah, I have a question," Harold said, "How much is this thing gonna cost? Just a half hour ago we heard the treasurer's report. We're already way beyond the budget. I don't see how we have a dime to spend on anything that isn't basic in this church. In fact, I'm surprised that we haven't started talking about reducing staff. So before we get started, I think we oughta know whether or not we're just wasting our time talking about something we can't possibly afford. How much is this gonna cost?"

The congregational meeting, especially Bob and his committee, just had a bucket of cold water dumped on them by an influential Christian with an unbiblical worldview. It happens in churches everywhere. God lays plans for his people of faith to do his work, only to have them set aside because of the cost. This shows us a window through which we can understand how God's abundance—not finances—determines the possibilities.

Henry Blackaby recounts a powerful personal experience in his life as a pastor in his book, *Experiencing God*. In it, he demonstrates that cost is not nearly as critical a factor as faith and obedience. He participated in an association of churches committed to making an impact on the World's Fair at the Expo center in 1986. They had a total income of about $16,000, but as Blackaby indicates, the circumstances of their income was irrelevant compared to the power of prayer.

"As an association of churches, we decided that God had definitely led us to the work that would cost $202,000. That became our operating budget. All of our people began praying for God to provide and do everything we believed he had led us to do during the World's Fair. At the end of the year, I asked our treasurer how much money we had received. From Canada, the United States, and other parts of the world we had received $264,000.

People from all over came to assist us. During the course of the Fair, we saw twenty thousand people come to know and trust Jesus Christ as Savior and Lord. You cannot explain that except in terms of God's intervention. Only God could have done that. God did it with people who had determined to be servants who were moldable and remained available for the Master's use."[1]

How you trust God's abundance determines your possibilities. God is much more powerful than financial figures on a spreadsheet. When God leads you to take a risk, is it responsive in faith? Or does the cost factor prevent further exploration of God's calling? Are you called to be part of a church of action? Can you be challenged to take steps of faith and "remain moldable for the Master's use"? To be effective, you need to look through the window that focuses on faith in a God of abundance. It's a biblical window that can help you look at your finances in a whole new way.

A Matter of Sequence

For the numerous Christians excited about new training for reaching the lost, Harold's soliloquy drenched the anticipation. The question, "How much does it cost?" is not in itself a bad one. There are times when that question is relevant and there are certainly times when it is a responsible one to ask. But when it enters prematurely in the process, as Christians seek to discern God's will, it represents an unbiblical worldview. Is "How much does it cost?" a commonly asked question in your congregation? Do you ever ask it? God-inspired plans are often snuffed out by Christians who don't understand that God is limitless. God is the key to the possibilities—not how much money is in the checking account.

Imagine, once again, Jesus in heaven prior to his mission to earth. God the Father is explaining Jesus' mission. He's unfolding the way he chose for Jesus to redeem humankind. He begins with the virgin birth in Bethlehem. He explains the fulfillment of many prophecies through Jesus' birth.

Suddenly Jesus interrupts impatiently, turns to the Father, and says, "Before you go any further, how much is this gonna cost? How long will this take, and what will be the expense?"

The cost issue wasn't foreign to Jesus' thinking. After all, he's the one who taught the parable relating that it's wise before building a tower to first count the cost (Luke 14:28-30). There has to be a stewardship consciousness in the planning end of any strategic effort for God's work. But often, when the words, "How much does it cost?" are interjected early in the directional process, they represent a diabolical smokescreen that derails the mission that God has given you. The first question shouldn't be, "How much does it cost?" The first question should be, "Is God in it?" God pays for what he orders. Think about the opposite: something may be cheap, but if God isn't in it, do you really want it? It's much more effective to step out in faith and trust God to provide than to take a cheaper model that God didn't want. After all, you are on his mission to his world, and what God decides, God provides.

What God decides, God provides.

There is a *biblical* sequence for determining whether or not God is leading your church to start a program, hire a staff member, purchase a curriculum, plant a church, etc. Three key elements should be incorporated.

Vision

Vision is vitally important, but underused when it comes to evaluating what God is calling you to do. In your church, you can't rely on the merit of the idea alone. You have to sell it to the people. You have to help people look past the hang-ups. Many churches are financially weak because the leadership isn't casting a vision that sparks people to action. Casting a vision that creates excitement about what God is doing in your community is essential in helping others look past the cost, and past themselves. My friend Jim Manthei says, "Vision precedes provision."

Prayer

Instead of discounting an idea because of the price tag, pray for God's leading. Give God room to move, and the cost might not end up as a crucial factor. God doesn't give assignments without providing the resources.

Details

After casting a vision and calling out to God in prayer, you'll have a better idea of whether or not God is in it. If he is, then the details follow. Cost can be discussed, but it won't be nearly as intimidating as before.

The God of Abundance

Budget time can be a tense time at church. Will you be willing to risk a little and stretch for God? Will you trust God's limitless desire to provide blessings by raising your giving by a percent or two? Will you wait to see what God wants to do instead of what you want? Finances go a long way toward dictating what a church is willing to attempt, but that's not how God wants you to react. He wants you to see him, not your circumstances. People who don't understand that God is a God of abundance will be less likely to risk anything for God because they're looking through an unbiblical window. If you don't honor God's desire to bless, you'll be unlikely to demonstrate a faith that takes risks.

> If you don't honor God's desire to bless, you'll be less likely to demonstrate a faith that takes risks.

I once pastored a church where many of the members would actually become excited around budget time. Sometimes there was a fair amount of stretch, but I still remember the buzz about the opportunities we felt God had given us to make a kingdom impact. That's because many in the congregation believed that God is a God of abundance.

The unbiblical window of letting finances dictate the possibilities reflects unbelief—God can't be trusted. The tendency to store up security for ourselves is also a demonstration of unbelief: God is limited. But the Bible consistently shows that God is a God of abundance—not scarcity. God doesn't have a dwindling supply room from which he rations out blessings to his people. On the contrary, God is beyond limitations and he pours his blessings onto those who have the faith to trust him. How can a God who promises to "throw open the floodgates of heaven and pour out so much blessing that you will not have room enough for it," be a God with limitations? If God can make a promise like that, then why do so many Christians live as if God's supply is running out? Why do so many churches let their view of finances frustrate God's work? The biblical window is clear: God is not a God of scarcity. He is a God of abundance.

By the Numbers

In examining the statistical analysis, refer back to the last chapter, which conveyed that only one in four of the Christians in churches we surveyed give a biblical tithe of 10% or more. Not only does a lack of biblical stewardship bind up what God wants to do in the world, it also perpetuates a false assumption among believers and non-believers that God doesn't bless most churches! Our research shows that almost

FIGURE 6A
ALMOST HALF GIVE LESS THAN 5% OF THEIR GROSS INCOME
TO THE WORK OF THE LORD THROUGH THEIR CHURCH

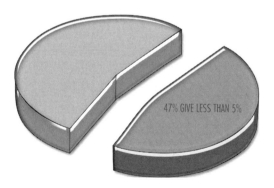

47% GIVE LESS THAN 5%

half (47%) give less than 5% of their gross income to the work of the Lord through their church. In research interviews we discovered that many active Christians misunderstand the abundance of this crucial biblical promise—you can't outgive God! This severely handicaps God's mission work because it contributes to the lack of funds in their church. What percentage do you give?

Crowd Reaction

I've been in churches where the treasurer is one of the most anticipated speakers. The members listened politely to what the pastor had to say, but really sat up to hear if there was any money in the church's bank account. In one instance, the treasurer was extremely worried. He was sweating, his voice was shaking, and his hands were trembling. He announced to the congregation, "Well, all the bills are paid, but there's almost no money left in the account." I know he was anxious about how the church would react, but I honestly wanted to stand up and clap! If churches are faithfully using their money to fulfill the main purpose of the church, then why should they be worried about finances? If there's ministry happening, needs being met, people meeting Jesus, and disciples being made, churches won't have to worry about going under. God blesses those who trust him, especially when his followers are following his lead and letting him determine the possibilities.

> *Churches stagnating with wealth*
> *are churches in danger.*

Churches stagnating with wealth are churches in danger. There are more churches like this than you might imagine. In their meetings, the treasurer might say, "Well, the bills are paid, and we still have $42,000 left over." The members nod in satisfaction, content that the church's affluence is secure.

Doesn't that sound ridiculous? If I was a member in one of those churches, I would stand up and say, "Forty-two thousand dollars left over! What *aren't* we doing? Who aren't we trying to reach? What ministries are we overlooking or underfunding? How can we spend that money to reach people who don't know Christ?"

Think back to how God provided for his people during the exodus. In the desert, God rained down manna for his people, but he gave them strict instructions not to hoard it. The people were to take only enough for that day, and leave the rest. He was teaching life by faith. Those who didn't obey found that the manna decayed and became worthless after a day. Storing up for the days ahead wasn't a part of God's plan.

God wants you to trust him with your finances day by day. He calls you to be receptive to his leading and his mission. He challenges you to value obedience over financial security, and to remember that he is a God of plenty—not a God of limitations. Instead of asking, "How much does it cost?" you should ask, "Is it God's will?" God's math is different from secular math because God's math says that the more you give, the more you receive. If you are spending on God's will, he will always provide, because he truly is a God of abundance. And if he's in charge of everything, he's in charge of your finances too. Why wouldn't he supply your needs when you are doing what he wants?

If churches are spending on God's will, he will always provide, because he truly is a God of abundance. Why wouldn't he supply your needs when you are doing what he wants?

Are You Hiding?

What if Jesus were to come back and visit a church that had a surplus of funds in their account? What if outreach ministries were suffering because the leaders felt it would be wiser to place money in "reserve" funds? What if lost people were not being reached because the church was saving instead of strategizing? What would he say?

The Bible indicates that Jesus was not an advocate of stockpiling resources. In Matthew 25, he tells a parable that speaks directly to the issue of using God's blessings instead of hoarding them. In the parable, a boss gives three of his servants different sums of money. He leaves, trusting the servants to make the money work for him in his absence. Two of the servants, who were given five and two talents respectively, fulfill the boss's directive and double their money. The other servant, who was given one talent, dug a hole and hid the money. When the boss returns, he commends the first two servants and severely disciplines the one who hid the money. In fact, he calls him a wicked and lazy servant (Matthew 25:26, 27). With that, he takes away his money and throws him out.

Some churches are tempted to hide their talents while the master is away. But God has made us the managers of his world, and Jesus clearly shows that God won't tolerate hiding money in the ground—or, more aptly, a bank account.

Now, what if Jesus were to come back today and find no money in the church's treasury? The money all went to ministering to the community, underwriting programs on Christian radio, allotting money to start new ministries, and sharing the good news of salvation through Christ. What do you think he'd say then?

In the parable, Jesus says that the boss showered the other two servants with praise—"Well done, good and faithful servant . . . Come and share your master's happiness!" (NIV). God congratulates his people the same way. The key is to recognize God's blessings, and use them to carry out his mission.

Of course, I'm not advocating unwise spending, or racking up credit card debt to meet needs and then hoping for Jesus to return before the collection agency calls. I am challenging you to return to a biblical worldview that focuses on what God wants *first*. I'm challenging you to cast a vision to your church based on what you believe about God. People of great faith who believe God's promises look through a window of divine abundance that touches their own giving patterns. Then they carry that over to their influence in the church. In turn, they develop others and challenge them to study the Scriptures and check out God's assurance of an endless supply house for his work.

How you see your faith in God's abundance determines the possibilities. It's a window that reveals God's nature, God's promises, and God's blessings. Don't get mired in "How much does it cost?" Don't hide your talents in the ground. And above all: when you see God moving in your community, get on board and cast such a vision that the only way it will ever work is if God is in it!

When you see God moving in your community, get on board and cast such a vision that the only way it will ever work is if God is in it!

Lining up the Windows

Window 1:	Your Purpose Determines Your Mission
Window 2:	Your Comfort Determines Your Sacrifice
Window 3:	Your Image Determines Your Impact
Window 4:	Your Desires Determine Your Priorities
Window 5:	Your Blessings Determine Your Giving
Window 6:	Your Abundance Determines Your Possibilities

Getting a Better View

1. *Evaluate your own finances.* Ask yourself, "What is it that God wants me to do, that I'm not doing even though I have financial blessings?" Let God's work drive your need for resources, not resources determine God's work.

2. *Encourage the leaders of your church to present new ministries to the congregation* only when they are convinced God has ordered it. Teach leaders to process decisions with strong discernment, Scripture reflection, and prayer—before they're brought to congregational members. This will prevent those "Harolds" from dumping cold water on Christians who are enthusiastically doing God's work.

3. *Ask your leaders to focus on casting an effective vision—not on the details.* As a key leader in the church, your pastor should also be a visionary. Encourage other leaders to focus on vision. Those with the gift of leadership should be able to communicate with the congregation in an influential way.

4. *Ask those who are managers in your congregation—those with the gift of administration—to focus on the details.* This means that leaders should spend most of their energy determining if the vision is from God, and managers should deal with the details and business end of the spectrum. They should be the ones who ask, "How must does it cost"? Use a spiritual gift discovery tool to help those who are leaders and those who are managers discover and use their gifts.

5. *Focus on the reality that God is an abundant God, and not a God of scarcity.* Study the Scriptures that illustrate how God is not confined to limitations, but is more than able to provide for the world he created. Study the book, *Discipling Nations* by Darrow Miller in your small group.[2] Focus on the part of the book that talks about God being a God of abundance.

The Last Word

"Far better it is to dare mighty things, to win glorious triumphs, even though checkered by failure, than to take rank with those poor spirits who neither enjoy much nor suffer much because they live in the gray twilight that knows neither victory nor defeat."[3]

Teddy Roosevelt

"I can do all things through Christ who strengthens me."[4]

The Apostle Paul

Your Past Determines Your Future

"But that's not the way we've always done it."

Tradition or Traditionalism?

Pastor Brower, the senior pastor at Grace Community, had been spending a considerable amount of time praying about the annual church picnic. For years prior to his arrival, the church picnic had been a staple on the calendar. It began as an opportunity to increase the level of fellowship among the 100 or so members of the small rural church. But times had changed dramatically at Grace. Commercial development had occurred near the church, and several housing additions followed. Suddenly, more people were visiting and becoming members. When a Wal-Mart was constructed nearby, the church laid plans to build on a new site. The congregation jumped from 100 to 500. Assimilation challenges mounted. Staff members were added, and several new ministries were started. Somehow, the historical church picnic wasn't the fellowship experience it once had been. One Saturday afternoon, he gathered his group of key leaders to talk about it.

"Since our church has grown, we've become a church of many congregations. With three worship services, it's next to impossible for anyone to know everyone. Our staff ministers to so many newer people in different ways, even I don't know everyone by name anymore. That's why we've developed the infrastructure of small groups, and redesigned the Sunday morning Bible studies as fellowship groups. With God blessing us with growth as he has over the last few years, we've all realized that the "family feeling" of church is not really based on knowing every one, but knowing some.

Anyway, because of what we've put in place with the groups, it seems that it's not really necessary anymore to continue having a church-wide annual picnic."

Linda, the secretary, spoke up immediately, "But pastor, we've always had a church picnic. I began coming to this church as a child thirty-five years ago. There's been a church picnic the first week of July, every summer, ever since I was a little girl. I know attendance has somewhat dwindled and some who attend feel like they're meeting at the park with a bunch of strangers, but maybe we just need to work harder at it. I mean, when I think of great community, the church picnic is one of the things I think of."

Linda sees the church through the wrong window. Instead of focusing on its mission and ministry, its value and beliefs—things that never change—she's focused on the external things, which change—and must change—when they become worn-out roadblocks of traditionalism. How easy it is to make an idol out of the church picnic! How easily we attach ourselves to the past, refusing to let go. But it's impossible to be the church God wants us to be if we can't trade the past for the future.

Essentials and Non-essentials

The worship service had just ended, and Beth was obviously upset when she sat down to talk to Karen.

"I really don't like those drums in church. It seems like we're turning our worship service into a nightclub act. I don't see why we have to add these different instruments. I never grew up with those in church. You know, Karen, we hardly ever use the pipe organ anymore. What do we have it for? I can remember sitting in the pews as a kid and hearing the beautiful sound of the pipe organ. I'd like to have that feeling back again when I go to church. And the hymnal! What's with this stuff flashed up on a screen? When I think about worshipping in church, I think about holding the hymnal. I heard they're even thinking about removing the hymnals from the pew racks. It just doesn't seem like worship to me anymore."

"Yeah, I know what you mean," sympathized Karen, "you know, we have a lot of new, younger people coming to our church, who didn't grow up with the pipe organ or the hymnal. Isn't it exciting to see them in church? You know, Beth, life changes. Think about that computer screen. It wasn't that many years ago that you didn't know what the word Internet meant. Neither did I."

"But that's my point," responded Beth with some evident frustration in her voice, "our whole world is changing. Everything is changing so much. And the rate of change is accelerating. I go to church so I can get away from all that change. I'd like church to be that one area of life that just stays the same." *Message hasn't changed*

There are two constants in this world—and only two. Christ and change. The key is to have a finely tuned biblical worldview that separates the essentials from the non-essentials. The essentials are what we die for, non-essentials come and go. It's like that old phrase: "Methods are many, principles are few. Methods often change, principles never do." The key issue in the Christian faith is to distinguish between the form and the substance of the faith. Many of the traditions of the past are really non-essential, but because of their longevity or personal attachment, they become baptized as essentials. Concentrating on non-essentials takes time away from the essentials. Looking through a biblical window of change means you appreciate the past but develop ministry for the future, because how you see your past greatly determines your future.

Think of the stoning of Stephen in Acts 7. Why was the young evangelist stoned to death? If you look back in chapter 6, verses 11-14, you begin to see the context of the riot that ended his life. The religious leaders were going through the crowd and igniting their anger. And the platform of their concern? "This man never stops saying things against this holy place and the law; for we have heard him say that this

Jesus of Nazareth will destroy this place *and will change the customs that Moses handed on to us."* They had made gods out of their church building and religious practices. But these were never intended to be timeless axioms of the faith. Stephen was stoned because he claimed that Jesus would change the customs of Moses. The customs were expected to be followed in Moses' time, but Christ had changed everything! To the religious people they seemed comfortable, but Christ had declared them as non-essential. New wine required new wineskins.

Church buildings come and go. Customs are merely vehicles that allow spiritual experience. Like the car in your garage, vehicles for the faith change from time to time. They wear out! Upgrades come along. But the religious leaders who ignited the crowd against Stephen defined religion by their customs and buildings, not faith premises and God's promises. Tradition is the living faith of the dead. Hebrews 11 is an inspirational walk down memory lane. All those people—now dead—had a living, timeless faith that cheers on those who follow Christ. But the religious leaders who killed Stephen were caught in the trap of traditionalism—the dead faith of the living—a faith in customs and habits.

Present at Stephen's death was the Christian persecutor, Saul. Saul, too, was a proponent of preserving tradition at all costs. Later, he had a face to face encounter with Jesus on the road to Damascus. His life would never be the same. As a missionary to many different people, he recognized with clarity the difference between the essentials and the non-essentials. His training steeped him in both, but he recognized the flexibility of one and the steadfast adherence of the other. As pointed out in the Window of Priorities, Paul was willing to do everything necessary to lead others to salvation. Flexibility in methods is essential for effectiveness in mission. Paul's commitment to getting the saving gospel to people was non-negotiable. It was part of the tradition of truth that he would die for. But the means and the vehicle changed from group to group and from time to time. His strength was his worldview of clarity and the difference between tradition and traditionalism. He knew that how you see your past—the traditions and non-essentials—determines your future.

A friend of mine told me recently that as he was driving by his former church, he saw the same people talking to the same people, and probably having the same conversations that they had ten years ago. It was a church stuck in the past, and if they don't look through the biblical window of change soon, their future will just look like the past. I've met pastors who suffer from this. While their colleagues have gained thirty years of experience, they've had one year of experience thirty times!

Blind Leading the Blind

In Matthew 15, we see the Pharisees anxious to find Jesus. They had a serious bone to pick with him, and it wasn't the first time. Jesus had been eating and healing on Sabbath days. He was getting under the skin of these Jewish leaders. But this time they were all bent out of shape because of the behavior of the disciples. They weren't following the laws about washing their hands before eating. It was bad enough that the rebel was attracting a following and breaking the customs, but now his disciples were doing it! They strode right up to Jesus, because this was a staple of Jewish living based on interpretations and applications from the law of Moses—important stuff! Irritated and hopping mad, the Pharisees say in verse 2, "Why do your disciples break the tradition of the elders? For they do not wash their hands before they eat."

Jesus retorted from a different worldview. "And why do you break the command of God for the sake of your tradition?" (verse 3). Jesus confronted the Pharisees on their blatant hypocrisy. He knew that their love for tradition was more important to them than their relationship with God. He threw down the gauntlet by saying that they put their own agendas ahead of the will of God. The tradition of hand washing wasn't a God-given directive, but a decree from the elders. Because of the possibility of having touched something unclean during the day, Jews were advised to wash their hands before eating. It was practical advice to protect Jews from what they had touched. The Pharisees considered such decrees to be religiously binding.

This same religious chauvinism shows up in many churches today. It's found when Christians refuse to bury traditions that no longer serve a need. It shows itself when unchurched people sit in worship services, bombarded with terms they don't understand and rituals that don't make sense. New wine can't go into old wineskins.

Many churches alienate the unchurched in their community—the people they say they're trying to reach. While the members may be comfortable and happy, the main purpose of the church goes unfulfilled. In his confrontation with the Pharisees, Jesus took a firm stance against prioritizing tradition over reaching people for the kingdom. He concluded his argument as he spoke with the disciples. The disciples heard everything that Jesus told the Pharisees, and while they probably appreciated his defense, they were nervous. Wringing their hands they tell Jesus in Matthew 15:12, "Do you know that the Pharisees took offence when they heard what you said?" They were, once again, looking through a different window than Jesus. They weren't concerned about the content of the argument; only the repercussions—Jesus had made the Pharisees angry. Their worldview was tainted with wanting to look good, not make waves. But Jesus was sent to change those worldviews.

He says to them in verse 14, "Let them [the Pharisees] alone; they are blind guides of the blind. And if one blind person guides another, they will both fall into a pit."

Although the Pharisees were the religious leaders, Jesus recognized that their worldviews didn't coincide with the Father's. Because He valued doing the Father's will over honoring tradition, he challenged the disciples to leave the worldview of the Pharisees. The way they viewed their past was determining their future, and it was a road to nowhere. Old wineskins don't work for new wine.

By the Numbers

In this "by the numbers" section we look at two survey questions that reflect a Christians' perspective on eternity. This data provides clues that even active Christians can slip from faith in essentials to faith in non-essentials—shifting the focus from salvation through Jesus to salvation by works—what we do. The research shows that large blocks of active Christians rely on their works—customs and habits—rather than Christ for salvation. In our Spiritual Awareness Survey, we asked Christians, 81% of whom are weekly worshippers, "Have you come to the place in your spiritual life where you can say for certain that if you died tonight, you would go to heaven?"[1] A total of 84% of those surveyed indicated that they believed they would, 2.1% said that they did not believe they would, and 13.9% said they didn't know. Those numbers aren't nearly as shocking as the results from the next question. "Suppose you were to die tonight and God asked you 'Why should I let you into heaven?' What would you say?"[2] The possible answers are faith (trusting in Jesus Christ alone for salvation), works, and undecided.

FIGURE 7A
SUPPOSE YOU WERE TO DIE TONIGHT AND GOD ASKED YOU,
"WHY SHOULD I LET YOU INTO HEAVEN?"

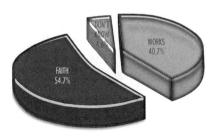

Four out of ten people surveyed rely on their own good works to receive eternal life! This is a complete contradiction to the way of salvation taught in the Bible. You can't find anywhere in the Bible that salvation comes through works. In fact, it says just the opposite. Paul says in Ephesians 2:8-9, "For by grace you have been saved through faith, and this is not your own doing; it is the gift of God—not the result of works, so that no one may boast." Addressing the crowd in Acts 4:12, Peter says, "There is salvation in no one else, for there is no other name under heaven given among mortals by which we must be saved."

Christians are constantly tempted to trust in themselves and their works rather than the truth of God, embodied in Jesus. This is one reason why it's so easy to slip into a worship of traditions. If you believe that you are saved by what you have seen and done, any change of those methods, customs, and celebrations is perceived as a threat to the way you believe you are saved. Your faith is in non-essentials—the traditions, the programs, and the rules. The Pharisees had this problem. They saw the new paradigm Jesus was intro-ducing into the world, but so relied on being right with God by what they did—they refused to change. They conspired to kill the agent of change. Salvation through Jesus Christ is essential. The order of worship is a non-essential—it can change. The annual picnic is not sacred. It can change. But for Christians with an unbiblical worldview related to the source of their salvation, the order of worship or the church picnic may be essential. As long as they're in worship, follow-ing the church calendar, or doing their religious thing, the subtle perception is that they're on the road to heaven. The statistics are too telling to deny. Four out of ten Christians, most of whom are weekly churchgoers believe they will receive eternal life through what they do and through what they have always done. They do not believe they are saved by the grace of Jesus Christ. That is one of the main reasons that traditionalism (the dead faith of the living) can subtly supercede tradition (the living faith of the dead).

An Eternal Lens

The preacher was in a dry spell. His spiritual fire had gone out. His heart no longer beat with a love for the lost. In desperation, he fell on his knees and cried out to God, "Please stamp eternity into both of my eyes!" Someone said, "If you want to keep eternity in perspective, analyze all things according to whether they're temporary or eternal." Cars are temporary. Houses are temporary. Bank accounts are temporary and so are church buildings. But neighbors are eternal. Relatives are eternal. Whether it's a postman, a mayor, a president, a cantankerous elder, or a grouchy bus driver, any human that lives or has ever lived is eternal. Bill Hybels sums it up quite effectively when he says, "You have never locked eyes with someone who doesn't matter to God."[3] Anything with eternal implications is important to God.

These are the essentials of life. The truths of God are the essentials of faith. Anything that is temporary is arbitrary. The difference is knowing which is which. The Window of Change helps you understand what to keep and what to retire because the past will not only greatly determine your future—but the futures of non-believers everywhere.

Lining up the Windows

Window 1:   Your Purpose Determines Your Mission
Window 2:   Your Comfort Determines Your Sacrifice
Window 3:   Your Image Determines Your Impact
Window 4:   Your Desires Determine Your Priorities
Window 5:   Your Blessings Determine Your Giving
Window 6:   Your Abundance Determines Your
　　　　　　　Possibilities
Window 7:   Your Past Determines Your Future

Getting a Better View

1. Develop a strategy that will help you focus on the difference between form and substance—essentials and non-essentials.

Clearly identify and label what are methods and what are principles, what can change and what can never change. Encourage this as part of the constant communication between the leaders of your church and the membership.

2. *Go to another Christian church that is different—a distinctly different denomination or tradition.* Or ask someone from that group to speak at your church. After hearing about their faith and their practice, ask the following question: Will they be with you and Jesus in eternity? So what is essential? What is not?

3. *Worship is one of the most visible and sensitive forms of Christian practice—*and often the hardest to change unless you have a clear worldview window. Study the different ways Christians have worshipped over the centuries, and how Christians in different countries and cultures worship. What are the universal principles? What are just the methods that change?

4. *Study the eleventh chapter of Hebrews.* Look closely at this chapter that describes many heroes of the faith who have lived and died—yet their faith lives on. This is a chapter that demonstrates the living faith of the dead. Contrast this with Jesus' constant battle with the Pharisees who often represented the dead faith of the living. Their faith was in the externals—the non-essentials. How would you characterize your church? Your own life?

5. *Create a climate of process in your church.* Talk often about change, experimentation, and flexibility. Emphasize that Christians have permission to try and permission to fail.

The Last Word

The Moravians provide this fantastic summary about what's important: "In essentials, unity; in nonessentials, liberty; and in all things, charity." I believe they have it right.

Your Pastor Determines Your Potential

"But isn't that what we hired the pastor for?"

Pastor Bernie

Pastor Bernie grew up watching his pastor. In fact, that's where he got most of his ideas about what pastors do and how they work. He saw his pastor work tirelessly. He remembers his pastor visiting him in the hospital when he had his appendix removed. He officiated at weddings and funerals. He visited and counseled people—basically did all the work of the ministry. He did all this and led three services each weekend. Very rarely did he ever take a vacation. At church suppers, they always called on the pastor to offer the prayer. It just seemed natural that the pastor was responsible for all the spiritual and ministry efforts around the church.

As he progressed through seminary training, Bernie didn't learn anything different. He never had a class on strategic leadership or empowerment. After ordination, Pastor Bernie became a pastor at a Lutheran church near the outskirts of town. Like his pastor, he too practiced a strong work ethic. He believed that biblical faithfulness included working hard without complaining. He never even considered equipping people to take up their role in ministry—even though he knew intellectually that the Bible teaches something like that. So Pastor Bernie makes all the hospital calls, visits the homebound and those in nursing homes. The members of the church cheer him on, pat him on the back each Sunday, and then return home while he spends the next few hours planning for Monday.

But Pastor Bernie is in trouble. He's constantly stressed, and he struggles with an increasing workload. People love the church and encourage others in the area to join. Now, more people need visiting, counseling, encouragement, and a listening ear. Pastor Bernie was twenty-six when he became a pastor. Now, he's forty-eight, and he doesn't have the energy he had when he started. He knows he's not getting the job done. But the greater challenge is that Pastor Bernie has discovered he is an enabler. He reinforces the spectator view of church. Without knowing it, Pastor Bernie is robbing God's people of the joy that comes from being a part of God's ministry. His church is far below its potential for mission and ministry and Pastor Bernie is starting to discover why.

Too many churches are like a football game. There are twenty-two people on the field desperately in need of rest and 80,000 people in the stands desperately in need of exercise. It's a sporting event. It's not the way God organized the church. Do you have a worldview that reflects the way God intends to accomplish ministry? Do you believe the minister is hired to do the work? Is that why there is staff? If there's more work, and churches can find the money, they add more staff. They operate far below their capacity to impact their communities. It's like a general pumping up his troops for battle—only to have him fight the war with a couple of assistants while the troops go home for chicken dinner. It doesn't make any sense! It's an unbiblical window through which many people evaluate the pastor—and it leads to pastoral burnout, ineffective ministry, and a spectator point of view. If you were in the hospital and, rather than your pastor, a trained volunteer visited and prayed with you, would you feel slighted? Would you wonder whether your pastor cared? Your answers reveal your window!

Mulitplication in Ministry

Tom was in a hospital recovering from lung surgery. It was about 6:15 p.m. when his good friend from church, Michael, arrived.

"How are you doing, Tom?" Michael asked.

"I'm still pretty sore from the surgery, but it gets better each day. I may get to go home tomorrow," Tom replied.

"That's great news!"

"Yeah. It's sure nice to see you, Michael. I've had a lot of visitors, and it's really made the time go by fast."

There was a long pause, and then Tom said something that had been weighing on his mind.

"The one thing that disappoints me, though, is that Pastor Jim hasn't been by. He phoned once and had a little prayer with me, but that was it. I really thought he'd come to see me."

Michael was a little astonished, and responded, "You mean no one from church came to see you? That's terrible! I can't believe no one from the church came to visit!"

Tom said, "No, it isn't that no one has come to see me. In fact, I've had an elder come each night. And, every afternoon, my Stephen's Ministry caregiver has come by. We've prayed and visited for just about an hour every day."

"Oh," said Michael, "I thought there for a minute that no one from church had seen you."

"On no, there have been plenty of people here. But I was really hoping that pastor would come by."

"Pastor Jim is leading a seminar today for other area churches. They're studying a new course that's supposed to help people become better witnesses for Jesus. Turnout is supposed to be pretty high," said Michael.

"Yeah, but isn't visiting the sick one of the things that pastors are supposed to do? How could he be so busy that he hasn't had time to come visit me? After all, that's what we're paying him for!"

Really? questioned Michael, privately.

Somewhere, Tom had missed the principle of multiplication in ministry. In Tom's business, he had practiced the concept of multiplication for years—and he was pretty successful. He had trained a sales force as well as representatives to serve as liaisons between manufacturers. He didn't meet with all the customers like he did when he started. His business was so big, and his responsibilities so broad, he couldn't! That's how he became so successful. But somehow, when Tom looked at the church, he looked through a different window. He saw the pastor as a hired hand—spiritually speaking. He felt the pastor was there to take care of people like him. Tom had never read Ephesians 4.

Ephesians 4 says that God has given *special gifts* to the church. Some of those gifts are called pastors and teachers. Others are called apostles, prophets, and evangelists. These gifts to the church are "to prepare God's people for works of service, so that the body of Christ may be built up." Those *special gifts* are given to the church to equip God's people—not just do ministry. It's God's strategy for multiplication. It's what moves the church from growth to explosion. It's the biblical key to the church's potential. It's what makes Christianity a movement, and it's why the Christian church has expanded globally. Unfortunately, it's not the way many Christians see the role of the pastor. Somewhere, the idea has developed that the pastor is there to serve them. After all, that's what they're paid for . . . right?

The window through which you see your pastor's role is extremely important, because the way you see your pastor determines the exponential potential of your church. If you expect your pastor to do it all in your church, then your church is probably well beneath its potential for kingdom impact. The potential is limited because the pastor is constantly performing maintenance tasks instead of leading the church.

The story is told of a man who went into a store and asked for a compass. The proprietor responded, "What kind of compass do you want? One that draws a circle or one that points the way?" There are really two kinds of churches and two kinds of pastors. Some are going around in circles, while others point the way. In what direction is your church headed? What role is your pastor playing in determining the direction? How is that related to how you see the role of the pastor?

Manager or Leader?

One of the roles of leadership is to cast vision and to convey the purpose and values of the church. Unfortunately, many pastors end up spending most of their time managing the church instead of leading it. This results in growth by addition, rather than multiplication through the equipping of others. In the first illustration at the beginning of this chapter, I described Pastor Bernie as one of those pastors who does it all. He carries all the burdens. What are the consequences? In his book, *Building A Contagious Church*, Mark Mittelberg writes, "Often the reality is that there is one person who is both pastor and minister, and then there are many helpers. These helpers are assigned to limited and often menial roles, while the pastor is dying while trying to keep up with all the real ministry functions. This approach will nearly (and in some cases, perhaps, *actually*) kill the pastor, and it will limit the quality and quantity of the ministry happening in and around the church."[1] Unfortunately, most pastors were never trained to see through this biblical window. When you look out the wrong window of leadership, you risk pastor burnout, apathy, and missing your potential.

By the Numbers

In our Mission Awareness Survey, we asked participants to identify the goal of the Great Commission. If you don't know the goal, then you probably don't really understand the mission.

Almost 40% answered correctly that the goal of the Great Commission is to go and make disciples of all nations. Here's the point: The biblical window calls for disciples—not church members. Disciples aren't spectators. Disciples are equipped to do the work of ministry. But only four in ten of the active Christians we surveyed see the goal of the church's work to be making disciples. That means that well over half of the Christians we surveyed identified the goal as preaching, teaching, and baptizing. In most churches, who is usually

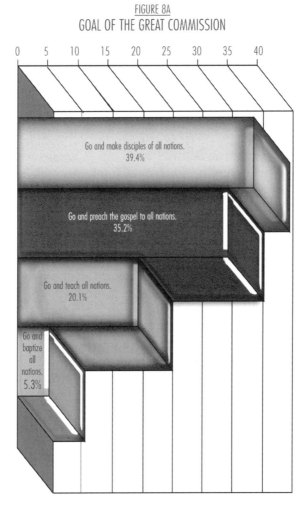

FIGURE 8A
GOAL OF THE GREAT COMMISSION

Go and make disciples of all nations.
39.4%

Go and preach the gospel to all nations.
35.2%

Go and teach all nations.
20.1%

Go and baptize all nations.
5.3%

responsible for the preaching, teaching, and baptizing? The pastor! Because 60% of the Christians we surveyed believe that the goal of the Great Commission relies on pastoral responsibilities, they make the pastor responsible for fulfilling the Great Commission.

God didn't call pastors alone to reach people for Christ—he called all Christians. He gives gifts as he sees fit to get everyone involved. It's God's blueprint for organizing the church. Churches that are moving forward and have a clear direction are the ones who have a church-wide minis-try—not just the ministry of the pastor.

By and large, most seminaries and Bible colleges don't teach the necessary principles of leadership, empowerment, or delegation. They encourage management of the church and purport the image that the pastor assumes all responsi-bilities. They train the pastor to carry out tasks that congre-gations deem worthy of a paycheck. But look at the statistics: H. B. London estimates that 1,300 pastors are leaving or being asked to leave their job each week! Pastors are getting burned out or fed up with the roadblocks that consistently impede their mission to reach people for Christ.

When I wrote my dissertation in graduate school, I stud-ied hundreds of pastors. I asked them to rate, on a scale of one through ten, what they thought was most important from a group of ten ministry categories. Most ranked evan-gelism—reaching people for Christ—as number one. Then I asked them to reflect on their schedules. As I evaluated how these pastors spent their time, energy, and gifts, almost every one gave the least amount of time from those ten areas to evangelism. Why does this occur? It occurs because members in many congregations don't look through the biblical win-dow of Ephesians 4 so the pastor is not seen as an equipper, but a doer of ministry. To many, the pastor is *their* pas-tor—called to meet their needs and handle their concerns. Even when the pastor knows that he or she should be train-ing others to make a greater impact, meeting the needs of the congregation subtly becomes a higher priority on the sched-ule. They're like the pastor who was training a student on marriage counseling. In their private meeting with a hus-band, the pastor would answer everything with, "You're right, you're so right." In the following meeting with the wife, the pastor again answered all her complaints with, "You're right, you're so right."

After she left, the poor, confused student said to the pastor, "How could you agree with the husband, and then take sides with the wife on the same issues?"

The pastor shook his head, sighed, and said, "You're right, you're so right."

Outside the biblical window, pastors are redirected from empowering people to caretaking. The church moves from mission to maintenance.

Get the Body Involved

Pastors who try to meet the congregation's needs by themselves are bound for endless frustration, self-doubt, and a constant lack of time to meet those needs. That's why God didn't design the church that way! Think about your own body. Did you know that countless forms of bacteria are present in your body at any given moment? Your body is constantly fighting off diseases, and it does so with the aid of your immune system. It's your immune system that sustains health and keeps you from becoming ill. At times, your immune system can't keep up with the harmful agents in your body, and you get sick. That's when you visit your doctor, who prescribes a treatment plan.

The body of Christ is designed to handle problems in the same way as your body. The members of the church are the immune system. Problems occur in churches all the time—whether it's a broken copier, a broken marriage, or broken trust. The members of the church, according to the gifts that God has given, can be part of the cure. The pastor's role is to equip, empower, and release the members for ministry toward one another . . . and to reach the world.

Exodus 18 gives an example of what happened to Moses when he tried to do it all himself. All day long the people would bring their cases before him, leaving him time for practically nothing else. When his father-in-law, Jethro, visited him, he recognized right away that Moses' method of leading the people was ineffective. The Bible even notes that everyone else *just stood around* (verse 13). Jethro advised Moses to train those around him to hear cases, but if a case arose that was beyond their ability to handle, Moses would hear it. Moses took Jethro's advice, and trained others to judge. Freed from that consuming duty, Moses was free to fulfill his appointment from God as the leader of the children of Israel. When Moses was free to be the leader he was designed to be, he had the valuable time to seek God and his will for his people. Out of that time with God, Moses was able to set the direction for the Israelites. Samuel Johnson said, "A man may be so much of everything that he is nothing of anything." What would Jethro say if he were to visit your church and witness the daily routine of your pastor?

When the pastor is the equipper of other believers, there is higher potential for outreach. Instead of equipping one person at a time, the church is able to send an army out into the mission field. As equipped believers grow, they train others in outreach. This is why the use of the term "exponential growth" is appropriate. That is a church with an enormous sending capacity.

Many pastors are so busy running the church that their prayer lives run the risk of stagnation. How can a pastor lead the church without seeking God's counsel on how to do it? Your church needs a kneeling pastor, not a running pastor. I tell pastors, "You don't have to die for the church, Jesus already did. And if you do, don't expect to be raised again in three days. And if you are, don't expect it to have nearly the same impact." It's true! A busy pastor isn't always an effective pastor. My friend Brad Benbow says, "Never confuse effort with results." I can tell you firmly: your pastor needs your help. Unless you look through the biblical window of multiplication through equipping, your pastor will be pressured into prioritizing maintenance over mission—because the way you see your pastor strongly determines the potential of your church.

Lining up the Windows

Window 1:   Your Purpose Determines Your Mission
Window 2:   Your Comfort Determines Your Sacrifice
Window 3:   Your Image Determines Your Impact
Window 4:   Your Desires Determine Your Priorities
Window 5:   Your Blessings Determine Your Giving
Window 6:   Your Abundance Determines Your
             Possibilities
Window 7:   Your Past Determines Your Future
Window 8:   Your Pastor Determines Your Potential

Getting a Better View

1. Study Ephesians 4 and learn of God's plan for multiplication by equipping others. Look at the roles of those in leadership positions, and ask yourself how they equip your members to do ministry that will enable your church to reach its potential.

2. Get all the leadership resources you can for your pastor. There are excellent books, tapes, and videos available. Make sure your pastor and leaders subscribe to magazines like *Rev., Strategies For Today's Leader,* and *Leadership Journal.* Pave the way for your pastor to attend at least one leadership conference or seminar per year. Encourage other leaders in your church to attend as well.

3. Evaluate your pastor's schedule. What does he or she do that could be done by somebody else? Encourage your pastor to start thinking in terms of training others to carry out tasks they are gifted to do. Open up more time on your pastor's schedule for prayer and study. What about your own schedule of Christian service? Who are you equipping right now? Who is your "project" of discipleship?

4. Study the strategic style of that great missionary, the Apostle Paul. Notice that Paul started churches in various towns, but as soon as one was started, he turned the ministry over to a leader he had trained. Study his letters to Timothy and Titus. How did he mentor them to lead the church, and not to manage it?

5. *Guide the leaders in your church to study the following books on leadership: The 21 Irrefutable Laws of Leadership* by John Maxwell, *Coaching Change* by Tom Bandy, *Missionary Methods: St. Paul's and Ours* by Roland Allen, *Leading Your Church To Growth in the 21st Century* by C. Peter Wagner, *The Purpose Driven Church* by Rick Warren, *Leaders* by Warren Bennis and Burt Nanus, and *The Power of Vision* as well as *The Second Coming of the Church* by George Barna. All are exceptional books that can help your pastor and leaders learn, develop, and employ valuable leadership skills.

The Last Word

I once heard D. James Kennedy say during one of his *Evangelism Explosion* conferences, "It is more important to train a soul winner than to win a soul." With a doctorate in theology, my first response was, "Heresy!" But the more I listened to what he had to say, the more it made sense. As you witness, have someone by your side, and train them as well. Multiply your ministry. That experience created a worldview shift in my life that I'll never forget.

Your Giftedness Determines Your Involvement

"We're looking for someone willing to put their name up for elder so we have a full slate."

A Misplaced Minister

I first heard about Mrs. Schneider from the parents who had children in her Sunday School class. The parents, many of whom had been around the church for quite some time, had endured Mrs. Schneider when they were kids. They basically told their kids, "If we can make it through, you can too." Mrs. Schneider's class had become an endurance gauntlet that gauged the commitment level to staying in the church. When I came along as Mrs. Schneider's new pastor, I asked her how it was that she began teaching Sunday School. She told me an incredible, sad story. Fifty years before, a young lady who was teaching Sunday School was having a baby. She needed a few months of maternity leave. The Sunday School superintendent asked Mrs. Schneider to fill in for a few months while the lady was gone. She agreed, and here she was, teaching Sunday School fifty years later! As we got to know each other, I asked if she had ever participated in a spiritual gifts discovery exercise.[1] Of course, she hadn't. I already knew she didn't have the gift of teaching. So did every child that had been in her class over the last half century! But when she did discover her gifts, she showed extraordinary dominance in the areas of service and mercy. It was then that a nursing home in our area began pleading with local churches to provide a ministry to those who lived in the home. I asked Mrs. Schneider if she would "retire" from

107

teaching Sunday School and lead the ministry to the nursing home. The sigh of relief from the Sunday School department could be heard for miles—not just from the students and parents, but also from Mrs. Schneider. As she developed her new ministry and began developing others, the lives of the nursing home residents and Mrs. Schneider were brighter—and so was our Sunday School. It was a Christian career change.

The real tragedy of that true story is the fact that the institution (the church) had a need, and without any sensitivity to God's creative work in Mrs. Schneider, or any perspective on how God energizes and activates people in the church, that congregation had institutionally abused her as well as the students she taught for five decades! It's disrespectful to God's plan and instructions—an abomination of the biblical window of how the church is organized. It's not only evident when Christians are drafted into service, it also happens when elections decide who serves in the church.

Mobilizing God's Army for Service

Dan and Joe were on the phone talking about the nominations committee. "Sorry to have to bug you with this, but pastor's twisted my arm on this one, Dan. I have to put together a slate of names for an election. I need to get an elder on the ballot, and I was wondering if you'd agree to have your name on it. You wouldn't have to do much, and I don't think it would take much time. Would you agree to run?"

Dan thought for a moment, and said, "Well, Joe, I'm flattered, but . . . I'm not sure I'm qualified. How do I know if I can do it"? Joe responded, "Check your pulse! Just kidding. Dan, we're just looking for names right now, hoping to fill the slate."

Not only is this a low view of Christian service, and an insult to the integrity of God's work, it's a worldview approach that is unbiblical on at least two levels. First, it ignores God's distribution of spiritual gifts. Second, the approach is wrong. It's driven by an institutional need rather than personal fulfillment of the individual.

You see, God does not *need* us. He *chose* us—so we can experience fulfillment. Jesus said, "I have said these things to you so that my joy may be in you, and that your joy may be complete....You did not choose me but I chose you. And I appointed you to go and bear fruit. fruit that will last, ..." (John 15:11, 16). When the Lord uses you to produce fruit with eternal consequences, you will experience fulfillment with divine dimensions.

The previous chapter showed the biblical worldview of pastors serving as leaders and equippers, as opposed to hired hands who do all the work while everyone else cheers. This chapter is to encourage you to look through a biblical window that shows how God has designed your church. He's created a team by divine design—not a form of government where workers are slotted by elections, drafting, or guilt trips.

In the case of Mrs. Schneider, she had been drafted to serve temporarily, and then never released to find her true calling in the church. She was asked to fill an institutional need. In the case of Dan and Joe, the church didn't consider seeking out individuals by matching spiritual gifts and passions. Instead, they wanted to put names on a ballot for voting. Earlier, I mentioned Acts 6 as a reference to how the New Testament church was becoming mired in maintenance. With all the needs of the widows they were serving, the leaders of the church were losing ground in getting the gospel message out to lost people. So what did they do? Did they have an election? No. Did they grab any warm body available? No. Instead, they chose those who were "full of the Spirit and of wisdom" (Acts 6:3). They didn't just choose anybody who had extra time. One of those men was Stephen, who I referenced in the Window of Change. In Acts 6:9-10, we see further confirmation that Stephen had this spiritual gift, for it says, "Then some of those who belonged to the synagogue . . . stood up and argued with Stephen. But they could not withstand the wisdom and the Spirit with which he spoke." Wisdom was necessary for deciding how to serve the widows in the best way, and Stephen had that gift. By doing this, the apostles expanded their team, which freed them up to lead the church.

Paul wrote to the Corinthians, "Now concerning spiritual gifts, brothers and sisters, I do not want you to be uniformed" (1 Corinthians 12:1). He taught them about God's design for the church. He then proceeded to list the various gifts.

Paul understood a Spirit led church, with God's fingerprint on each Christian's place of service. He didn't advocate popularity contests to determine how needs would be filled, nor did he teach that vacancies should be filled with any warm body available. Relying on a governmental structure for the church is inefficient and unbiblical. The Spirit's ministry of gifts is God's way to organize the church.

The key is to make sure that everyone has an opportunity to discover their gifts and get involved. In China, every male serves in the army for two years. There are few exceptions. One man who enlisted in the army was born without arms. He basically thought, "What in the world can I do"? The supervising officer brought him over to where another man was sitting beside a water pump. The officer said, "This man here pumps the water into these buckets. Your job is to tell him when the bucket's full. He's blind." The enlisted man's question had been answered. Everyone can do something.

King David said, "I am fearfully and wonderfully made. Wonderful are your works; . . . " (Psalm 139:14). God doesn't make junk. He never created anything that didn't have a purpose. He empowers you to serve in areas that fulfill you, impact others, and make kingdom contributions. Feelings of inadequacy evaporate when you look through the biblical window. How you see your giftedness determines your involvement.

The Commodity of Time

Discovering your spiritual gifts is one important part of this process. The other is being motivated to commit your time to serve in your area of giftedness. Many believe that money is the most valuable commodity on this planet. I disagree. The most valuable commodity is time.

Don't believe me? Try hanging out at any airport on a Friday evening. It's almost always packed, and the airplanes are usually oversold. As the airline agent picks up the microphone, the bidding war begins to entice someone to give up their seat and take a later flight. First, the agent might offer a $200 voucher, good toward a ticket to anywhere their airline flies. That's a lot of money, but few take it. Next, the agent might offer a free, round trip ticket. Most of the passengers in the lobby don't even blink. Higher and higher the stakes go, until the right number of people give up their seat.

Some of those offers equate to over $500! So why do most people keep their seat? It's because they value their time more than the money. When I'm in that kind of situation, I want to get home and see my wife and kids! It may seem like only a few extra hours in the airport, but that crucial time could be invested in my family. Many others guard their time the same way. Bernard Berenson said, "I would willingly stand at street corners, hat in hand, begging passersby to drop their unused minutes into it." Time is a resource you can't stockpile.

How does this relate to your church? Your time is one of the critical investments of your life—and you can't put it in the offering plate! In God's kingdom, your time may be more valuable than your money. Think about a church that has a lot of money, and resides in a beautiful cathedral. What good is it if everybody's too busy to share the gospel, lead the church, grow spiritually, minister to the poor, serve the elderly, or challenge the spiritually dead? However, even if a ministry is constantly scraping bottom, renting facilities, and barely getting by, yet it has energized people who touch others—that work will be blessed. God uses people to reach people. Time commitment is essential for eternal production. Maybe you tithe your money. Do you tithe your time?

By the Numbers

In our surveys, we asked "Do you volunteer through your church?" Of the responses tallied, 43.6% said that they volunteer regularly, and 48.1% said they do so once in a while. The percentage of respondents who said they never volunteer through their church was 8.3. Those numbers signify that many churches operate well below their potential. It doesn't have to be that way, and it wouldn't be if everyone in the church saw God's personal plan for their fulfillment through the biblical window of giftedness.

Have you ever been asked to serve but responded, "I just don't have time?" Have you overlooked God's blueprint for Christian involvement and service?

FIGURE 9A
SUMMARY OF THOSE WHO VOLUNTEER THROUGH THEIR CHURCH

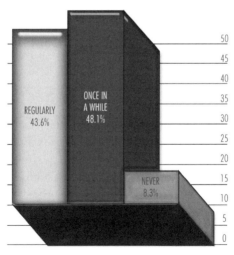

I've never met anybody who has fifty-two hours in their day. Five minutes doesn't last longer for one person than it does for another. The issue isn't the amount of time you have, it's how you use it. The key is to reevaluate your priorities. Instead of watching a TV sitcom that you'll forget a few days later, you could set aside that time specifically for service. How it's done depends on how God has gifted you. There are 168 hours in every week. Health experts recommend an average of eight hours for sleep, so that knocks the number down to 112. Most people work a forty to forty-five hour week, so taking the high end would reduce the number to sixty-seven hours. If 10% of that time was tithed, the amount of time dedicated for service amounts to approximately six and half hours. It still leaves plenty of time for family involvement, maintaining your living space, entertainment, Bible Study, and everything else in your life. But you also make a valuable contribution to God's work. Just as financial stewardship isn't giving "to the church," neither is the tithing of time. It's returning a portion back to God, who creates time for all people. What if most Christians began tithing their time? In a small congregation of 100 people, that would be over 600 hours per week! If only half of the congregation tithed their time, that would still equate to over 300 hours. Pastors would be less tempted to draft people into service. Elections could disappear—there would be no reason to have them! Churches could experience the excitement of continually starting new ministries to different people. Even beyond the church, that time is still God's. He may lead Christians to serve in the community—at soup kitchens, shelters, or clinics. You can't put time into the offering plate, but you can still make it count.

Putting the Plan into Action

Opportunities to serve in your church pop up all the time, but you may not always be the one to serve. In a person-centered recruitment process, the way God has gifted you determines whether you should be in that area of service. There are five steps to follow when ministry opportunities arise. Consider the following scenario, and ask yourself what your response would be.

"Janet, would you help us with Vacation Bible School? We need someone who's good with children, and we're wondering if you'd take one of the classes in the program."

The first thing that runs through Janet's mind is, "What will it cost me?" Not a bad question, but it shouldn't be first.

Five Questions in Their Proper Sequence

1. Accomplishment? "What will it accomplish?" What kind of return on the investment will this be for the kingdom of God? Businesses are generally known for having a results-oriented point of view. Most Christians don't think in terms of results. But if Janet's not proceeding with a goal in mind—namely, accomplishment for the kingdom of God—then she's not starting at the right place. It's important to evaluate what kind of impact your service will make, and if that's the kind of impact that God wants.

2. Gifted? "Am I uniquely gifted to do this work"? Would your spiritual gifts contribute well to this ministry? If Janet has the gift of leadership and teaching, then asking her to paint the nursery may not be the best stewardship of her gifts. However, teaching a Vacation Bible School class could utilize her giftedness with a large return for the kingdom through her investment of time.

3. Someone else? "If I do this, will I hinder someone else from serving in their area of giftedness"? Will you be restricting others who will "sit on the bench?" Availability to God is important, but it's also wise to discern when God may be trying to get someone else involved. If Janet is the "go to" person all the time because she makes herself available, others might never step up. Younger people, or new members with the corresponding gifts, could be challenged to get involved first.

4. What should I give up? "What else do I do that may be a lower priority that I can set aside?" How can you maximize ministry without stretching yourself thin? If Janet believes that God plans to use her to reach children through the Vacation Bible School, then she needs to evaluate what else she does in ministry. If she's also serving in several other areas, it may be necessary to train someone else to fulfill one of those responsibilities.

5. Expense of time and energy? "How much time and energy will this require for me to do a top quality job?" Do you have enough time and energy available to do this the right way? In her heart, Janet may really want to teach the class, but if she's overly committed in other areas, she may not be able to serve with excellence in a way that would honor God. It may be necessary to alter her schedule or recruit someone else to teach the class.

Career Change

Career changes are more prevalent than they used to be. Almost everyone makes a career change at some point. It creates excitement and brings freshness to the occupational mindset. The same principle applies in Christian service. I've seen greeters without the gift of hospitality, elders without the gift of knowledge, and caregivers without the gift of encouragement. Like Mrs. Schneider—she agreed to serve in a specific area to fill a void and didn't have the opportunity to serve somewhere else for years. Have you ever felt that God has called you to a different area of service? If so, I strongly advise you to make a career change in your church. Let the way God has designed you determine how you serve—not the needs of the institution. Start by discovering your spiritual gifts—but don't stop there. Discovering your gifts is only half the process. Find areas of ministry where you can use those gifts.

Unwrapped Gifts

Imagine that it's Christmas morning, and you're a kid again. As soon as you wake up, you rub your eyes, rush down the stairs, and dash into your living room. Under the Christmas tree are all sorts of presents, each wrapped in different styles of paper. You can make out some of the shapes, but not all of them. You turn around, and there your parents stand, smiling as you gaze upon the presents. What do you next? Would you turn on the television and ignore them? I doubt it! More than likely, you'd tear through the wrapping paper as quickly as seven-year-old fingers can, anxious to see what's underneath. God has given gifts to all his children, and no Christian should leave those gifts unwrapped. You may be able to make out the shapes of some of your gifts, but you'll never know what's underneath if you don't unwrap them. Your giftedness determines your involvement.

Lining up the Windows

Window 1:   Your Purpose Determines Your Mission
Window 2:   Your Comfort Determines Your Sacrifice
Window 3:   Your Image Determines Your Impact
Window 4:   Your Desires Determine Your Priorities
Window 5:   Your Blessings Determine Your Giving
Window 6:   Your Abundance Determines Your Possibilities
Window 7:   Your Past Determines Your Future
Window 8:   Your Pastor Determines Your Potential
Window 9:   Your Giftedness Determines Your Involvement

Getting a Better View

1. Purchase the audiotape Activating Members For Ministry, available from Church Doctor Ministries. Listen to it, and share it with your friends at church. Discuss the difference between person-centered and institutionally-centered recruitment.

2. *Evaluate the structure of your church.* Is it an institutional organization? Do you often hear your pastor pleading with people from the pulpit to fill vacancies? Are members ever encouraged to start new ministries? Encourage your leaders to recruit people based on their areas of giftedness instead of filling a gap.

3. *Is it the time in your life to consider a Christian career change?* Personally discuss this with a friend or two. Evaluate whether or not you're in the area of your giftedness. Get counsel to find your place of fulfillment.

4. Study how you use your time. What gets the highest priorities? Commit to tithing a percentage of your time to your church. Encourage others in your church to do the same.

4. *If your church doesn't have a system in place for educating your members about spiritual gifts, make it a priority to start one.* I highly recommend the workbook, *Gifted For Growth*, available from Church Doctor Ministries. It not only guides you through the spiritual gift discovery process, but it also leads you into ministry. It can help you get on the road to fulfillment and effective service for God. I would also recommend *Network* (available from Willow Creek Community Church). Encourage your church leaders to make spiritual gift training and assimilation a part of the new member process. This includes children! Ask the leaders to develop a database that represents every member in your church—with their spiritual gifts. Your leaders can refer to it when ministry opportunities arise.

The Last Word

During World War II a church in Germany was bombed. The statue of Christ in the courtyard was severely damaged.

Both hands were broken off. Instead of replacing the hands, the congregation placed a sign on the statue which read, "You are my hands."

The Power of God Determines Your Attitude

"It can't be done."

Is Pessimism Christian?

I once pastored a small, rural church in northeast Indiana. When I arrived, I found a discouraged group of people with incredibly low corporate self-esteem. The church had suffered a split a few years earlier, and with all the finger pointing, membership decline, and constant turmoil, they were barely surviving. Their condition was critical. I sensed the need for a small victory—something to begin building esteem momentum. So I developed a vision that had a focus on the future—not their difficult past. As I looked at the facilities, I noticed that the building itself looked depressed. It was one of those white framed country churches, but the paint was peeling on all sides. It gave the appearance of a discouraged church. My challenge to them was to put vinyl siding on the church. It required raising $18,000—more than any project they had accomplished in quite some time. But I felt that such an accomplishment would lift their spirits and give them a victory to build on for the future. They would see that when God is in something, anything can happen. Their attitude would brighten.

It was Lloyd—Mr. Negative—who came up immediately (and publicly) and said, "It can't be done." As I think back, based on the financial giving record of Lloyd, I'm not surprised he felt that way. He showboated so well, everyone thought he was a generous giver!

When I first heard Lloyd's reaction, I was quite naïve. I figured he must have had a logical reason behind his objection. So I tried to learn from him. Then I tried to argue and debate with him. I learned later that dealing with Lloyd meant dealing with his worldview—which had been negative since his childhood. Said a farmer in the congregation, "Lloyd has been a contrary person ever since I met him . . . in first grade."

Is pessimism a Christian worldview? Can a person be a Christian and pessimist both? Frankly, I don't see how! After all, if you look to the end of Scripture in Revelation, you can learn something quite significant: we win! No wonder the Apostle Paul said, in the spirit of a Christian worldview, "We know that all things work together for good for those who love God, who are called according to his purpose" (Romans 8:28). Or what about when he said, "I can do all things through him who strengthens me" (Phil. 4:13)? Jesus promised, "Ask, and it will be given you; search, and you will find; knock, and the door will be opened for you. For everyone who asks receives, and everyone who searches finds; and for everyone who knocks, the door will be opened" (Matthew 7:7-8).

All Things Are Possible

I love the story of the preacher who had an unexpected miscue while he was preaching on the feeding of the five thousand. He boldly announced, "And Jesus fed a few people with five thousand loaves of bread."

Jack, who was a cantankerous sort of person, spoke up from the fourth row before the pastor could correct himself: "Well that's no miracle, even I could do that!"

The next week, the preacher was determined to get the story straight and put one over on Jack. So he told the story right. "Jesus took five loaves of bread, and two fish, and fed five thousand people." Then the preacher paused, looked at Jack, and said, "Jack, I bet you couldn't do that!"

But Jack was quick, "Sure I could. I'd just take the food that was left over from last week."

My wife is a preschool teacher. One day she also taught the story of Jesus feeding the five thousand. After telling the children that the disciples passed out all the food, she said, "So what do you think happened next?"

One little boy didn't miss a beat. He said, "Then they passed out the cookies!"

You see, for that little boy, nothing was impossible for God. In fact, it was easy for him to believe that God would top off such a miracle with cookies! It was Jesus who said we should have faith like children. He also said that if we have faith as large as a tiny mustard seed, we can tell a mountain to jump in the sea, and it will. In Genesis 18, God told Sarah that she, in her old age, was going to give birth to a son. The Scripture says, "So Sarah laughed to herself, saying 'After I have grown old, and my husband is old, shall I have pleasure?'" (verse 12). Her attitude was negative because she didn't understand the power of God. So God turned to Abraham and said, "Why did Sarah laugh, and say, 'Will I really have a child, now that I am old?' Is anything too hard for the Lord?" (verses 13-14, NIV).

Imagine if every Christian understood challenges and circumstances within the framework of God's claim: "Is anything too hard for the Lord?" Creating the universe and everything in it wasn't too hard. Destroying every living creature on the earth with a flood, save a few, wasn't too hard. Neither is raising the dead, saving people from an eternity in hell, or sustaining a relationship with his chosen people for thousands of years. Yet, when challenging situations arise in the church, some Christians who claim they believe in this same God are quick to say, "It can't be done." Despite all this evidence to the contrary, pessimism often takes a strong foothold. Pessimistic people see the glass half empty instead of half full. The sky is partly cloudy instead of mostly sunny. Their negative attitude can infect the whole church. What is it that you see out your window?

Jesus had the right idea about what is possible and what isn't. But, throughout the New Testament, his disciples needed work. Remember the rich, young man who asked Jesus what he should do to inherit eternal life? Jesus told him he needed to sell all his possessions, give the money to the poor, and then follow him. The man went away sad, because he had a lot of money, and had no desire to part with it. Seeing this, Jesus turned to his disciples and said, "Truly I tell you, it will be hard for a rich person to enter the kingdom of heaven. Again I tell you, it is easier for a camel to go through the eye of a needle than for someone who is rich to enter the kingdom of God" (Matthew 19:23-24).

This created problems for the disciples. Jesus was changing their worldview again, and it involved their eternal salvation. They began to worry. The Bible says, "When the disciples heard this, they were greatly astonished and said, 'Then who can be saved?' But Jesus looked at them and said, 'For mortals it is impossible, but for God all things are possible'" (Matthew 19:25-26).

Jesus embodied what the Scriptures say in Genesis 18, that nothing is too hard for the Lord. What is impossible for humans is possible for God. Remember—he is a God of abundance, not a God of limitations. Jesus reflected the power of the Father with the attitude, "God can." If you look at God through some other window, you won't recognize that power. You'll reason, "God can't." You'll look at your circumstances, finances, outreach, obstacles, or your church through an unbiblical window, and you'll say, "It can't be done. We can't do it."

Famous Can's and Can't's

The Bible is filled with stories of people who either believed God is who he says he is, or didn't believe that God could get the job done. Here are a few examples.

Famous Can's

Gideon (Judges 7)

Imagine God sending *you* to battle the Midianites with 32,000 troops. You'd probably feel secure. Now imagine that God decides to send you with 31,700 troops less than when you first set out! Would you cry, "It can't be done"? Gideon didn't, and his faith was rewarded with a thorough defeat.

Joshua (Joshua 6)

"March around the city for six days? Priests with rams' horns? Walls collapsing by themselves? What's going on? That's no way to take out a city!" What if that had been Joshua's response to God's plan for the fall of Jericho? God would have been looking for a new general! But Joshua did as God commanded, as odd as it may have sounded. Jericho fell. Joshua let his worldview about God determine his attitude toward God's plan.

The Centurion (Matthew 8:5-13)

Faith isn't based on sight, so the centurion who asked Jesus to heal his servant wasn't expecting Jesus to come to his house. He firmly believed that Jesus was who He said He was—and had the power of God. Jesus would only have to say the word, and the servant would be healed. Jesus was astonished at the centurion's faith, and the servant was healed immediately. This worldview is summarized in Hebrews 11:1, "Now faith is being sure of what we hope for and certain of what we do not see."

Famous Can't's

The Ten Spies (Numbers 13-14)

Although God had promised Canaan to the Israelites, ten of the twelve spies who surveyed the land didn't want to take it. There were giants living in the land. Instead of remembering God's promise and relying on his power, they focused on their own assessment of the situation. As a result, the people rebelled and were sent back to the desert. God often calls his people to venture into new territory. What about your response, and on what is that response based?

The Disciples (Matthew 14:13-21)

The disciples had seen Jesus perform miracles. But when Jesus told them to feed a crowd of five thousand men, they cried, "It can't be done!" They focused on their limited resources instead of the unlimited power of Jesus. Do you focus on limited resources, or the power of God?

Thomas (John 20:24-29)

He had heard that Jesus had risen, but he refused to believe. "Unless I see the nail marks in his hands and put my finger where the nails were, and put my hand into his side, I will not believe it" (John 20:25). Thomas had seen Jesus' body on the cross. It crushed his hope of a future. The power of God raised Jesus to life. Not even death can diminish the power of God.

By the Numbers

Isaac Singer said, "If you keep on saying things are going to be bad, you have a good chance of being a prophet."[1] Why does so much negativity come from Christians? I believe many don't really understand who God is, what he has done, and what he does. Do you look through the right attitude window? Our Spiritual Awareness Survey asks, "Do you attend a regularly scheduled Bible class at church or in a home?" The question that follows asks, "Do you have regular daily devotions?"

Billy Graham once said that many Christians are biblically ignorant. How well do you know the character of God? It's difficult to have a clear picture of the power, love, faithfulness, generosity, and heart of God without learning about him through his Word. Half of the people surveyed are not developing a biblical understanding of God, beyond hearing a sermon. Do you assume limitations that aren't really true? Do you handicap God so he can fit in capsules you can understand? God is painted as not only limited in what he has, but also what he can do. Raise $450,000 for a Family Life Center? God can't do that! Yet Paul says in Philippians 4:13, "I can do all things through him who strengthens me," and Jesus says, "But for God all things are possible" (Matthew 19:26).

FIGURE 10A
PERCENTAGE OF THOSE WHO REGULARLY ATTEND
A SCHEDULED BIBLE CLASS AT CHURCH OR IN A HOUSE

PERCENTAGE OF THOSE WHO HAVE REGULAR DAILY DEVOTIONS

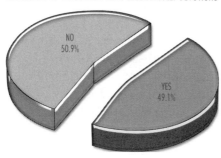

Jesus said something truly amazing when he said, "Very truly, I tell you, the one who believes in me will also do the works that I do and, in fact, will do greater works than these. . . ." (John 14:12). What a source of optimism! Do greater things than Jesus? Yes, as a matter of fact, we can—and we do. It's hard for me to fully grasp that my radio program, The Church Doctor^tm, is heard on hundreds of Christian radio stations, Monday through Friday. Let's imagine that I speak to over a million people a day, which is possible. Jesus, in his earthly body, could never have spoken to that many people at one time in a single day—let alone five days a week, every week of the year. On a typical day in the office, I'll get a telephone call from London and an e-mail from Sydney. How could we be pessimists, living in a world with the opportunities that we have? This is the most exciting time to be involved in ministry in *history*.

It seems to me, that among all people on earth, Christians should be those most filled with hope. We have an all-powerful God who has guaranteed Christians an eternity in heaven, through Jesus Christ. Tim Uecker once told me, "You can survive a month without food. You can survive a few days without water. You can survive a few minutes without air. But you can't survive a second without hope."

Martin Luther said, "Everything that is done in the world is done by hope. No farmer would sow one grain of corn if he did not hope it would grow up and become seed; . . . no merchant or tradesman would set himself to work if he did not hope to reap the benefit."[2] He understood that hope in God is not in vain. This is an important biblical window because how you see the power of God shapes your attitude about what can and can't be done. It also shapes your attitude toward the world in which you live. Is the world going to get better? Will world evangelization happen? Will your atheistic neighbor respond to the faith? Will your church ever reach its potential? Can a book like this really stimulate, with God's help, a biblical worldview that can change your life—and your friends, your small group, your leaders, and your church? It all depends on how you see the power of God. If you believe he is who he says he is, your attitude will reflect your faith. Nothing will be impossible for you, or your church. How you see the power of God determines your attitude.

Lining up the Windows

Window 1:   Your Purpose Determines Your Mission
Window 2:   Your Comfort Determines Your Sacrifice
Window 3:   Your Image Determines Your Impact
Window 4:   Your Desires Determine Your Priorities
Window 5:   Your Blessings Determine Your Giving
Window 6:   Your Abundance Determines Your Possibilities
Window 7:   Your Past Determines Your Future
Window 8:   Your Pastor Determines Your Potential
Window 9:   Your Giftedness Determines Your Involvement
Window 10:   The Power of God Determines Your Attitude

Getting a Better View

1. Study the promises of God. Let the Bible teach you why a Christian worldview is positive. Make sure you're in the Bible regularly. The more you discover God's ability to do anything, the more you'll be willing to step out in faith. Get to know God and His character better. It will affect your attitude.

2. Challenge negative thinkers—consistently, politely, privately, and firmly. Consider the possibility that they need to be evangelized. Their negative attitude may be the result of a lack of hope—which comes from a weakened or non-existent relationship with Jesus Christ. Don't allow them to influence other members of church with their negative thinking. Read John Maxwell's *The Winning Attitude*, and obtain the audiotape, *Attitude: The Difference That Makes A Difference.* You can be positive without disregarding reality.

3. Is your worship joyful and upbeat? Does it convey a spirit of optimism? The atmosphere of your worship says a lot about how you see God's involvement in His world. It's impossible to see God at work, and not get excited. Focus on a living, working, and limitless God.

4. Develop the "sandwich" style for correcting negative people in your church. Follow the Apostle Paul's method of beginning with thanksgiving and praise, follow with correction, and end with encouragement and exhortations. Help others understand this method of correction. It allows for the issue to be addressed, but it does it in a loving way.

5. Negative and pessimistic people should never be in positions of influence. Little motivation takes place if leaders are always saying, "It can't be done." Pacesetters in your church should be people who believe God is who he says he is, and if he is in something, it's going to work!

The Last Word

"Faith is a redirecting of our sight, a getting out of the focus of our own vision and getting God into focus. . . . Faith looks out instead of in and the whole life falls into line."[3]

A. W. Tozer

Lining Up the Windows

These ten biblical windows work in any culture, in any place, in any century. This is your time. Focusing on and operating out of biblical windows will lead you to spiritual effectiveness and fulfillment. As you interact with other believers and empower them to look through different windows, you get a glimpse of how biblical truth can shape lives. It will also shape your church to be a powerful force—accomplishing the mission of reaching people for Jesus Christ.

The Window of Purpose Identifies the Mission

With Jesus Christ's Great Commission transcending all other purposes and missions, you have a clear focus to evaluate all other programs, activities, events, church staff, messages preached, campaigns, and decisions. As issues arise in your life, you can measure them against God's purpose for you. This magnifies your God-given, personal mission and clarifies your struggles.

The Window of Comfort Models the Mission

When your mission is to make disciples, you will find yourself venturing into new territory on a continual basis. Life gets exciting! Reaching lost people will stretch you to leave your comfort zones. You'll grow and become all that God has planned for you. Jesus promises that it's worth the effort. His joy will be in you, and your joy will be complete. "I can do all things through Christ," said the Apostle Paul. You too can soar to new heights of obedience and sacrifice by the power of Christ. As this window impacts others around you, your church will stretch to accomplish the mission of making disciples. Your community will join you to marvel at what God can do.

The Window of Image Advances the Mission

With biblical windows one and two firmly in place, you are ready to go public! When the mission is defined as making disciples, and comfort is no longer a driving force, there's nowhere to go but out! You'll advance the mission by finding and meeting needs in your community. In the process of meeting those needs, you'll have opportunities to share the gospel with non-believers. Joining with others at church, you will project the image of friendly, compassionate, healthy, and lively believers who attract people to the message of Christianity.

The Window of Priorities Keeps the Mission in Focus

As you meet needs and reach people with the gospel, conflicts will arise. Some of your friends at church may feel dissatisfied with particular changes. Others may want to advance their agenda over the main purpose of making disciples. Your biblical window of priorities will keep the mission in front of you during tough times. Your Christian maturity will help you rise above the squabbles. What you want won't be as important as what God wants. This window lines up with the previous three windows because it helps you turn away from selfish motives. As this spreads among others, God's purpose remains clear and focused. Together, we want whatever God wants.

The Window of Stewardship Fuels the Mission

Money is God's fuel for the mission. Without it, ministry can't reach out into the community with significant impact. The biblical window of proportionate giving can free you to fund ministries that meet needs and share the gospel. When you invest your resources in the Lord's work, you'll have opportunities to reap the rewards of efforts that have eternal consequences. As you share this window with others, you'll influence some big picture people who will contribute to kingdom work, and fuel the mission in big ways.

The Window of Financing Gives Wings to the Mission

When you witness God's amazing work in the lives of people you reach, you'll be less tempted to veto ideas based on cost. By asking, "Is God in it?" instead of "How much does it cost?" you will trust the God of abundance and buy into his mission. As others at church look through this window, you'll collectively demonstrate faith in this God of abundance who will cast God-sized visions with unparalleled rewards.

The Window of Change Affirms the Mission

With the mission clearly in focus, and a worldview that rises above comfort, you take the ministry public and meet needs. You will function in an atmosphere of exciting change. While you will face some opposition to change, the mission becomes the clarifying factor of whether or not a change needs to be made. If proposed change is needed to accomplish the mission, then the mission is affirmed when the change is made. When this window influences others at your church, a clearer distinction between essentials and non-essentials will bring the power of focus to the mission of making disciples.

The Window of Leadership Multiplies the Mission

As you extend God's work into your community, you'll clearly see that your pastor cannot be responsible for meeting every need. Biblical leadership is all about equipping the people in your church to do the work of ministry. Not only is your pastor able to set the direction for the mission, but he or she will be equipping an army of ministers which multiplies the impact on the community. Instead of one individual leading the charge to make disciples, you and many others from church will be empowered to meet needs and reach people for Christ. As you equip others, you will multiply yourself.

The Window of Teamwork Individualizes the Mission

The biblical window on spiritual gifts offers you the opportunity to serve in your own area of God's work. At church, this heightens the number of individuals who become involved. It also increases the number of specialized ministries. This, in turn, enables your church to meet more needs and reach more people. As the Holy Spirit works through you and other members in areas of giftedness, you'll individualize the mission and work toward results with divine dimensions. Work in your gift area and you'll find fulfillment like never before.

The Window of Attitude Puts Faith in the Mission

The window of attitude will give you the faith perspective of "God can." Despite problems, conflicts, and frustrations, you'll exercise faith in a God who pays for what he orders, does what he says, and uses people like you to accomplish God-sized dreams. Faith in the mission will enable you and your church to overcome anything with the help of God.

APPENDIX A

Church Doctor Resources

Books

A House Divided (co-authored with Bob Whitesel)
Confessions Of a Church Growth Enthusiast
Gifted For Growth
Foundations of Church Growth
Move Your Church To Action
Six Faces of the Christian Church
Your Church Has Personality

Audiotapes

10 Tips For Sharing Your Faith
A Call To Action
Attitude: The Difference That Makes the Difference
Activating Members For Ministry
Be Encouraged; We Win!
Beginner's Manual For Christian Service, The
Courageous Churches
Effective Leadership For the Church
Engaging Christianity
Equipped To Serve: Jesus' School Of Discipleship
God's Principles For Financial Empowerment
How To Design and Develop Fellowship Groups
Growing Church In the 21st Century, The
Leading Your Church Through Change
Manager Or Leader?
Mistakes: What Do You Do When You Trip And Fall?
One-On-One Witness
Personal Worship In A Digital Age
Plan To Die
Reaching Kids: The Challenging Millennial Generation
Sacrifice and Service: Finding the Balance
Self-Esteem: What You Do Or Who You Are?
Take the Plunge: A Short-Term Mission Adventure

Ten Keys To Rekindling Evangelistic Outreach
Time: Your Non-Renewable Resource
Two Kinds Of Leadership
Under New Management: Living A Christian Worldview
Vision: Discovering God's Version Of Your Destiny
The Window Of Sensitivity
Worship Beyond the Stained Glass Barrier
You're Gifted! You're Special!
Your Search For Eternal Significance
Your Tongue: Very Small, Very Powerful

Research Model

This research model was conducted through one-half-hour to one-hour interviews with 15,000 active Christians—most of whom attend church regularly. The research also included 18,000 questionnaires completed by active members of churches, 80% of whom worship four out of five Sundays. The field of research includes 219 churches from twenty-five denominations as well as independent churches in the United States and Canada. These congregations have partnered with Church Doctor Ministries consultation division and this research reflects a portion of the analysis conducted at the time.

Our thanks to those who participated in this research though consultations conducted by Church Doctor Ministries.

A

Abiding Savior Lutheran Church
Independence, MO

Aboite Lutheran Church
Fort Wayne, IN

Advent Presbyterian Church
Cordova, TN

Arlington Presbyterian Church
Arlington, TN

B

Bartlett Presbyterian Church
Bartlett, TN

Bethany Lutheran Church
Slidell, LA

Bethany Lutheran Church
Elkhorn, NE

Bethel Lutheran Church
Morton, IL

Bethel Lutheran Church
Middleburg Heights, OH

Bethlehem Lutheran Church
Roseville, MI

Bethlehem Lutheran Church
Crete, NE

Bethlehem Lutheran Church
Aloha, OR

Bethlehem Lutheran Church
Yakima, WA

Bethlehem Lutheran Church
Nekoosa, WI

C

Calvary Presbyterian Church
Marietta, GA

Calvary Lutheran Church
Lincoln, NE

Christ Lutheran Church
LaMesa, CA

Christ Lutheran Church
Indianapolis, IN

Christ Lutheran Church
Lincoln, NE

Christ Lutheran Church
Willoughby, OH

Christ Lutheran Church
Fort Worth, TX

Christ Community Church
Palm Springs, FL

Christ Memorial Lutheran Church
Affton, MO

Christ the Ray of Hope Lutheran
Church
Albuquerque, NM

Christian Life Center
West Milford, NJ

Church of the Isles
Indian Rocks Beach, FL

Collierville Presbyterian Church
Collierville, TN

Community Christian Church
Salisbury, MD

Community Church of Joy
Glendale, AZ

Community of Hope
Brecksville, OH

Concordia Lutheran Church
Toledo, OH

Concordia Lutheran Church
Nashville, TN

Cornerstone Christian Church
Brownsburg, IN

Cross of Christ Lutheran Church
Bloomfield Hills, MI

D

Dearborn Hills UMC
Lawrenceburg, IN

Desert Cross Lutheran Church
Tempe, AZ

Divine Shepherd Lutheran Church
Omaha, NE

E

East Bethlehem Lutheran Church
Detroit, MI

Emmanuel Evangelical Lutheran
Church
Kettering, OH

Emmanuel Evangelical Lutheran
Church
Milbank, SD

Emmanuel Lutheran Church
Aurora, IL

Emanuel Lutheran Church
New Haven, IN

Emmanuel United Church
Windsor, Ontario

Emmaus Lutheran Church
Denver, CO

Evangelical Lutheran Church of the
Good Shepherd
York, PA

F

Faith Lutheran Bible Church
Silverton, OR

Faith Lutheran Church
Napa, CA

Faith Lutheran Church
Denver, CO

Faith Lutheran Church
Troy, MI

Faith Lutheran Church
Lincoln, NE

Faith Lutheran Church
Seaside, OR

Faith Lutheran Church
Collierville, TN

Faith Lutheran Church
Huntsville, TX

Faith Presbyterian Church
Germantown, TN

Faith United Methodist Church
Logansport, IN

Family of Christ Church
Petoskey, MI

Family of Faith Lutheran Church
Houston, TX

Farmington Presbyterian Church
Germantown, TN

First Brethren Church
Elkhart, IN

First Christian Church
Canton, OH

First Church of God
Eaton, IN

First Church of God
Goshen, IN

First Church of God
Grove City, PA

First Congregational Church
Montgomery, IL

First Presbyterian Church
Dalton, GA

First Presbyterian Church
Kennett, MO

First Presbyterian Church
Paris, TN

First Presbyterian Church
Somerville, TN

First Presbyterian Church
Trenton, TN

First United Methodist Church
Crystal Lake, IL

First United Methodist Church
Elgin, IL

First United Methodist Church
LaPorte, IN

First United Methodist Church
Kalamazoo, MI

First United Presbyterian Church
Winterset, IA

First Wesleyan Church
Akron, OH

Fort Wayne Gospel Temple
Fort Wayne, IN

FourSquare Gospel Church
Springfield, OH

Friendship United Methodist Church
Bolingbrook, IL

G

Gloria Dei Lutheran Church
Spokane, WA

Grace Community Church
Toledo, OH

Grace Evangelical Congregational
Church
Lancaster, PA

Grace Fellowship Church
New Haven, IN

Grace Lutheran Church
Huntsville, AL

Grace Lutheran Church
Dodge Center, MN

H

Harbor Light Community Chapel
Conway, MI

Brookdale Church
St. Joseph, MO

Heavenly Host Lutheran Church
Cookeville, TN

Holy Cross Lutheran Church
Fort Wayne, IN

Holy Cross Lutheran Church
Wichita, KS

Holy Cross Lutheran Church
Towson, MD

Holy Cross Lutheran Church
Arlington, TX

Holy Cross Lutheran Church
Nederland, TX

Holy Cross Lutheran Church
Racine, WI

Holy Ghost Lutheran Church
Monroe, MI

Hope Lutheran Church
Seattle, WA

I

Immanuel Lutheran Church
Danville, IL

Immanuel Lutheran Church
Rock Island, IL

Immanuel Lutheran Church
Lawrence, KS

Immanuel Lutheran Church
Columbus, NE

Immanuel Lutheran Church
Broken Arrow, OK

Immanuel Lutheran Church
Mount Clemens, MI

Immanuel Lutheran Church
Kansas City, MO

Immanuel Lutheran Church
Houston, TX

K

King of Kings Lutheran Church
Omaha, NE

L

Light of Christ Lutheran Church
Federal Way, WA

Living Christ Lutheran Church, The
Arlington Heights, IL

Lutheran Church of the Ascension
Atlanta, GA

Lutheran Church of the Good Shepherd, The
Bourbonnais, IL

Lutheran Church of Our Redeemer
Evansville, IN

Lutheran Church of the Resurrection
Marietta, GA

M

Marion Mennonite Church
Topeka, IN

Messiah Lutheran Church
Prince Albert, Saskatchewan
Canada

Messiah Lutheran Church
Indianapolis, IN

Messiah Lutheran Church
Lincoln, NE

Messiah Lutheran Church
Kenosha, WI

Mt. Calvary Lutheran Church
Phoenix, AZ

Mt. Calvary Lutheran Church
Fort Wayne, IN

Mt. Comfort United Methodist
Church
Greenfield, IN

Mt. Hope Lutheran Church
Grayling, MI

Mt. Olive Lutheran Church
Omaha, NE

Munford Presbyterian Church
Munford, TN

N

New Creation Lutheran Church
Ottawa, OH

North Dade Community Church
Miami, FL

O

Our Redeemer Lutheran Church
Iowa City, IA

Our Redeemer Lutheran Church
Eau Claire, WI

Our Savior Lutheran Church
Detroit, MI

Our Savior Lutheran Church
Flint, MI

Our Saviour Lutheran Church
Hinckley, OH

Our Savior Lutheran Church
Portland, OR

Our Savior Lutheran Church
Tacoma, WA

Our Savior's Lutheran Church
Sioux City, IA

Our Savior's Lutheran Church
Midland, TX

P

Pacific Hills Lutheran Church
Omaha, NE

Peace Lutheran Church
Lombard, IL

Penasquitos Lutheran Church
San Diego, CA

Pilgrim Evangelical Lutheran Church
Wauwatosa, WI

Pilgrim Lutheran Church
Bellevue, NE

Pilgrim Lutheran Church
Ontario, OR

Pilgrim Lutheran Church
Houston, TX

Faith Lutheran Church of the Deaf
Spokane, WA

Pilgrim Lutheran Church
Green Bay, WI

Prince of Peace Lutheran Church
Leo, IN

Prince of Peace Lutheran Church
Racine, WI

Q

Queensway Cathedral
Toronto, Ontario
Canada

R

Redeemer Lutheran Church
Mountain Home, AR

Redeemer Lutheran Church
Enid, OK

Reformation Lutheran Church
Wichita, KS

Resurrection Lutheran Church
Detroit, MI

Resurrection Lutheran Church
Seattle, WA

Rolling Hills Community Church
Zellwood, FL

Royal Redeemer Lutheran Church
North Royalton, OH

S

St. Andrew's Presbyterian
Belle River, Ontario
Canada

St. Jacobi Lutheran Church
Jennings, MO

St. James Lutheran Church
Burnsville, MN

St. John Lutheran Church
Ocala, FL

St. John Lutheran Church
Idaho Falls, ID

St. John Lutheran Church
Green Valley, IL

St. John's Lutheran Church
Bakersfield, CA

St. John's Lutheran Church
Decatur, IL

St. John's Lutheran Church
Lexington, KY

St. John's Lutheran Church
St. Louis, MO

St. John's Evangelical Lutheran
Church
Chicago, IL

St. John Evangelical Lutheran
Church
Northbrook, IL

St. John Evangelical Lutheran
Church
Rockville, MD

St. Luke Lutheran Church
Olney, TX

St. Luke's Lutheran Church
Ann Arbor, MI

St. Luke's Lutheran Church
Federal Way, WA

St. Mark Lutheran Church
Omaha, NE

St. Mark Lutheran Church
Ada, OH

St. Mark Lutheran Church
Cleveland, OH

St. Matthew Lutheran Church
Houston, TX

St. Paul Lutheran Church
Lakeland, FL

St. Paul Lutheran Church
Mt. Prospect, IL

St. Paul Lutheran Church
Sterling Heights, MI

St. Paul Lutheran Church
Stevens Point, WI

St. Paul's Lutheran Church
Omaha, NE

St. Paul's Lutheran Church
Livonia, MI

St. Paul's Lutheran Church
Milan, MI

St. Paul's Lutheran Church
Ann Arbor, MI

St. Paul's Lutheran Church
St. Louis, MO

St. Timothy Lutheran Church
Tarpon Springs, FL

Salem Evangelical and Reformed
Church
Florissant, MO

Salem Lutheran Church
Fremont, NE

Salem United Church of Christ
Fort Wayne, IN

Shepherd of the Desert
Scottsdale, AZ

Shepherd Street United Brethren in
Christ
Charlotte, MI

Shepherd of the Valley Lutheran
Church
Santa Ynez, CA

Shepherd of the Valley Lutheran
Church
West DesMoines, IA

Shiloh United Methodist Church
Cincinnati, OH

Stutsmanville Chapel
Harbor Springs, MI

T

Tabor Lutheran Church
Pueblo, CO

Trinity Lone Oak Lutheran Church
Eagan, MN

Trinity Lutheran Church
Pine Bluff, AR

Trinity Lutheran Church
Panama City, FL

2. Walt Kallestad, *Entertainment Evangelism* (Nashville, TN: Abingdon Press, 1996), 81.
3. George Barna, *The Frog In the Kettle* (Ventura, CA:Regal Books, 1990), 228.
4. David Price, "Why Churches Are Creating Lifestyle Settings," *Strategies For Today's Leader*, Second Quarter, 2001.
5. Lee Strobel, *Inside the Mind of Unchurched Harry and Mary* (Grand Rapids, MI: Zondervan, 1993) 85.

Worldview 4: The Window of Priorities

1. Kent R. Hunter, *Move Your Church To Action* (Nashville: Abingdon Press, 2000).

Worldview 5: The Window of Stewardship

1. R. T. Kendall, *Tithing: A Call To Serious, Biblical Stewardship* (Grand Rapids, MI: Zondervan Publishing House, 1982), 13.
2. Waldo Werning, *Supply-Side Stewardship* (St. Louis, MO: Concordia Publishing House, 1986), 32.
3. Larry Burkett, *Your Finances In Changing Times* (Chicago, IL: Moody Press, 1975), 106.
4. Church Doctor Ministries has representatives available to lead Kingdom Investing Clinics.
5. Stephen A. Macchia, *Building A Healthy Church* (Grand Rapids, MI: Baker Books,1999), 198.

Worldview 6: The Window of Financing

1. Henry Blackaby and Claude V. King, *Experiencing God: Knowing and Doing the Will of God* (Nashville, TN: Broadman & Holdman Publishers, 1994), 41-42.
2. Darrow Miller, *Discipling Nations* (Seattle, WA: YWAM Publishing, 1998), 232.
3. Ibid., 232.
4. Philippians 4:13 (NIV).

Worldview 7: The Window of Change

1. These questions are excerpted from D. James Kennedy's evangelism training course, *Evangelism Explosion*.
2. Ibid.
3. Bill Hybels, *Becoming A Contagious Christian* (Grand Rapids, MI: Zondervan Publishing House, 1994), 22.

Worldview 8: The Window of Leadership

1. Mark Mittelberg, *Building A Contagious Church* (Grand Rapids, MI: Zondervan Publishing House, 2000), 134.

Worldview 9: The Window of Teamwork

1. Church Doctor Ministries has spiritual gifts surveys and scoring sheets available for purchase.
2. Carl Bornmann.

Worldview 10: The Window of Attitude

1. Alan Loy McGinnis, *The Power of Optimism* (New York, NY: Harper and Row, 1990), 131.
2. Walt Kallestad, *Wake Up Your Dreams* (Grand Rapids, MI: Zondervan Publishing House, 1996), 16.
3. A.W. Tozer, *The Pursuit of God* (Camp Hill, PA: Christian Publications, 1982), 83.